I0483500

SHADOWBOXES

COLORING BOOK

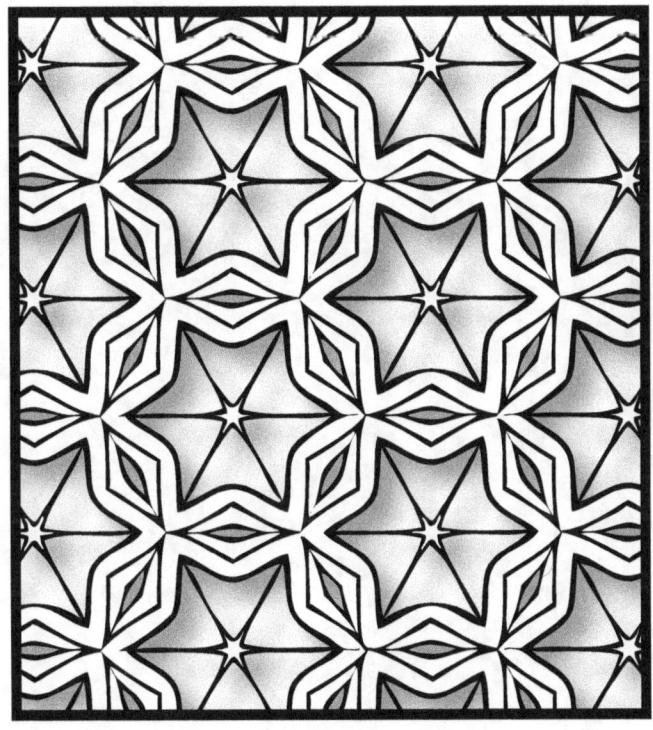

This book is printed on just one side of the paper
to avoid bleed through. If using markers it may be helpful
to place a piece of paper or cardstock behind the page.

To view samples of these illustrations colored by the author please visit
www.lovelyleisure.me

LOVELY LEISURE

ILLUSTRATIONS BY PAULA PARRISH

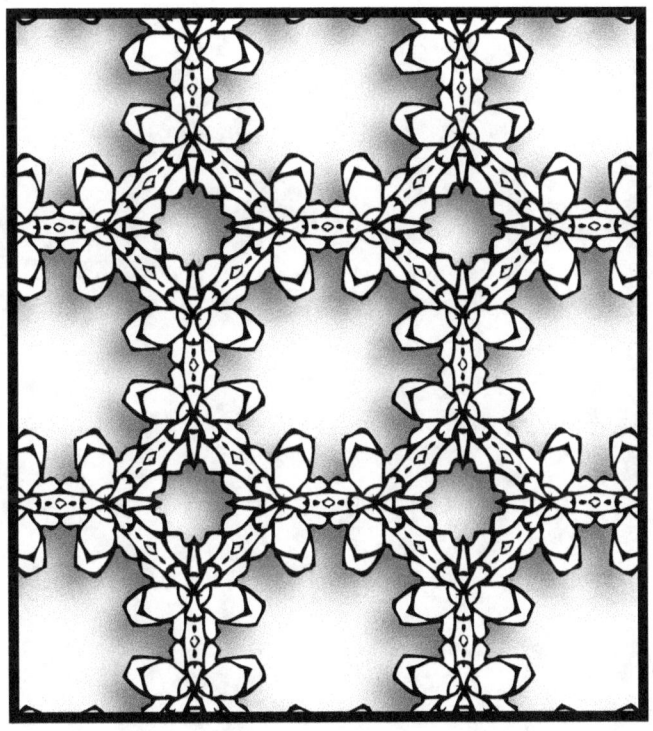

Shadowboxes Coloring Book
© 2016 Paula Parrish

www.lovelyleisure.me

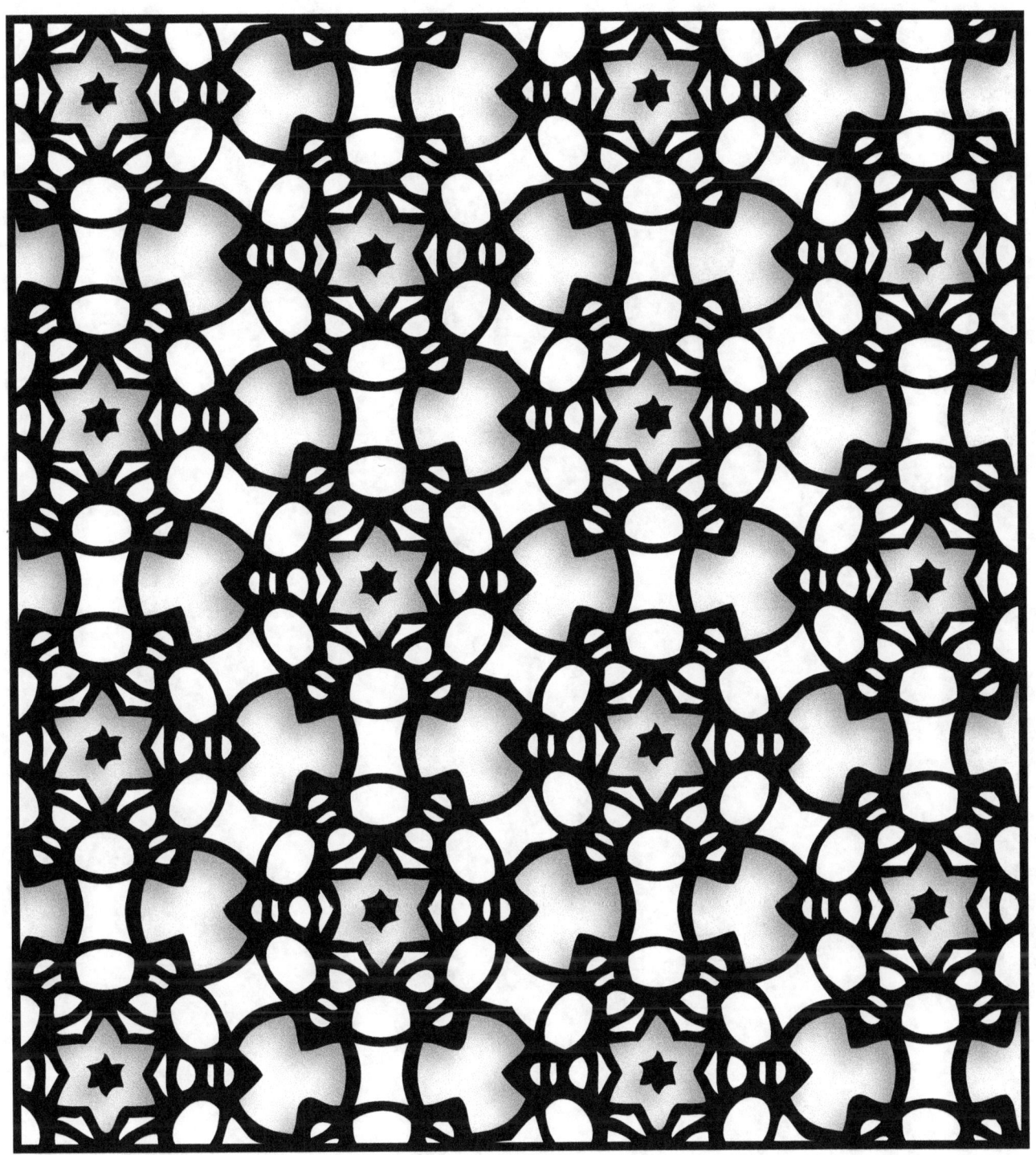

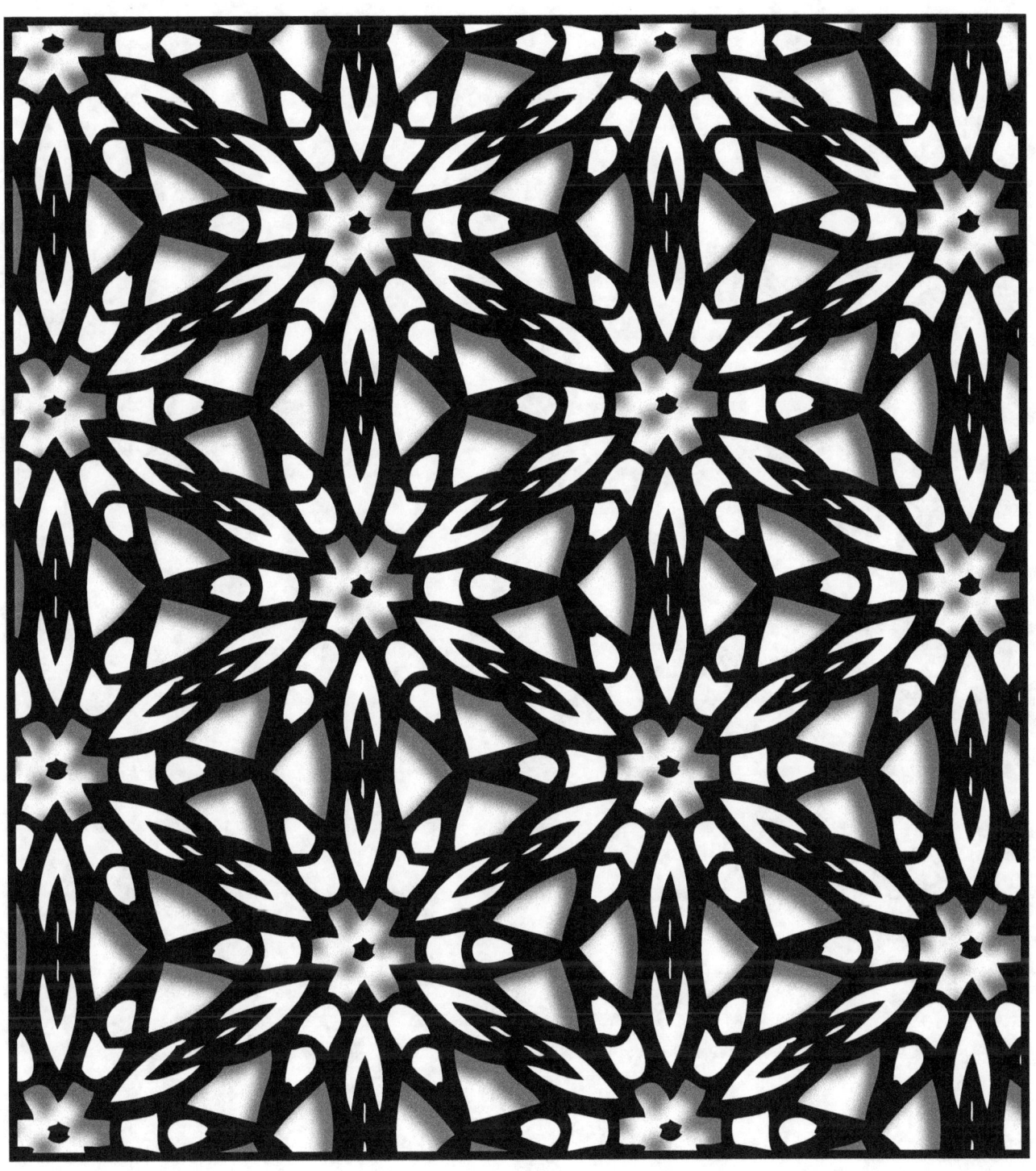

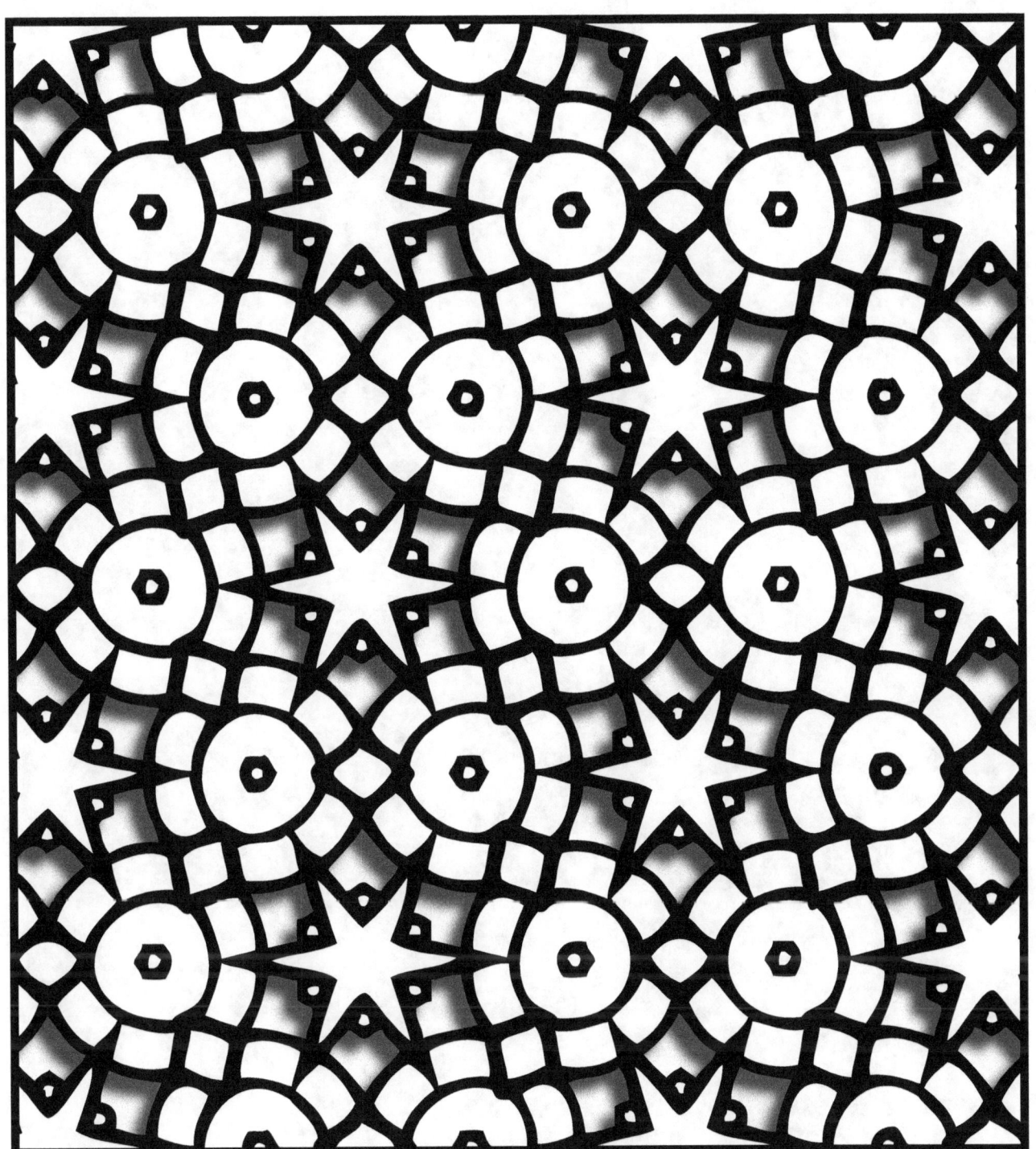

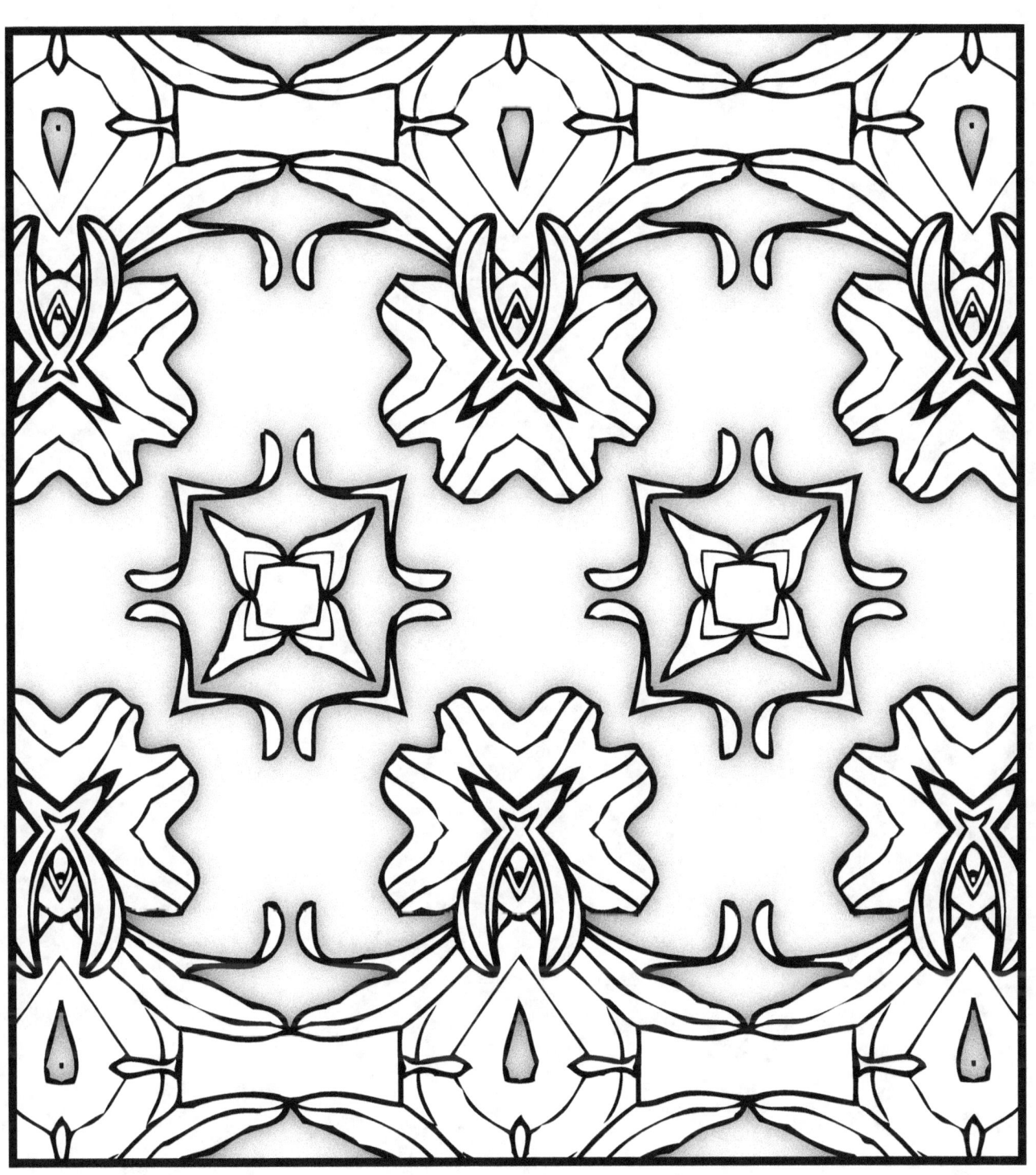

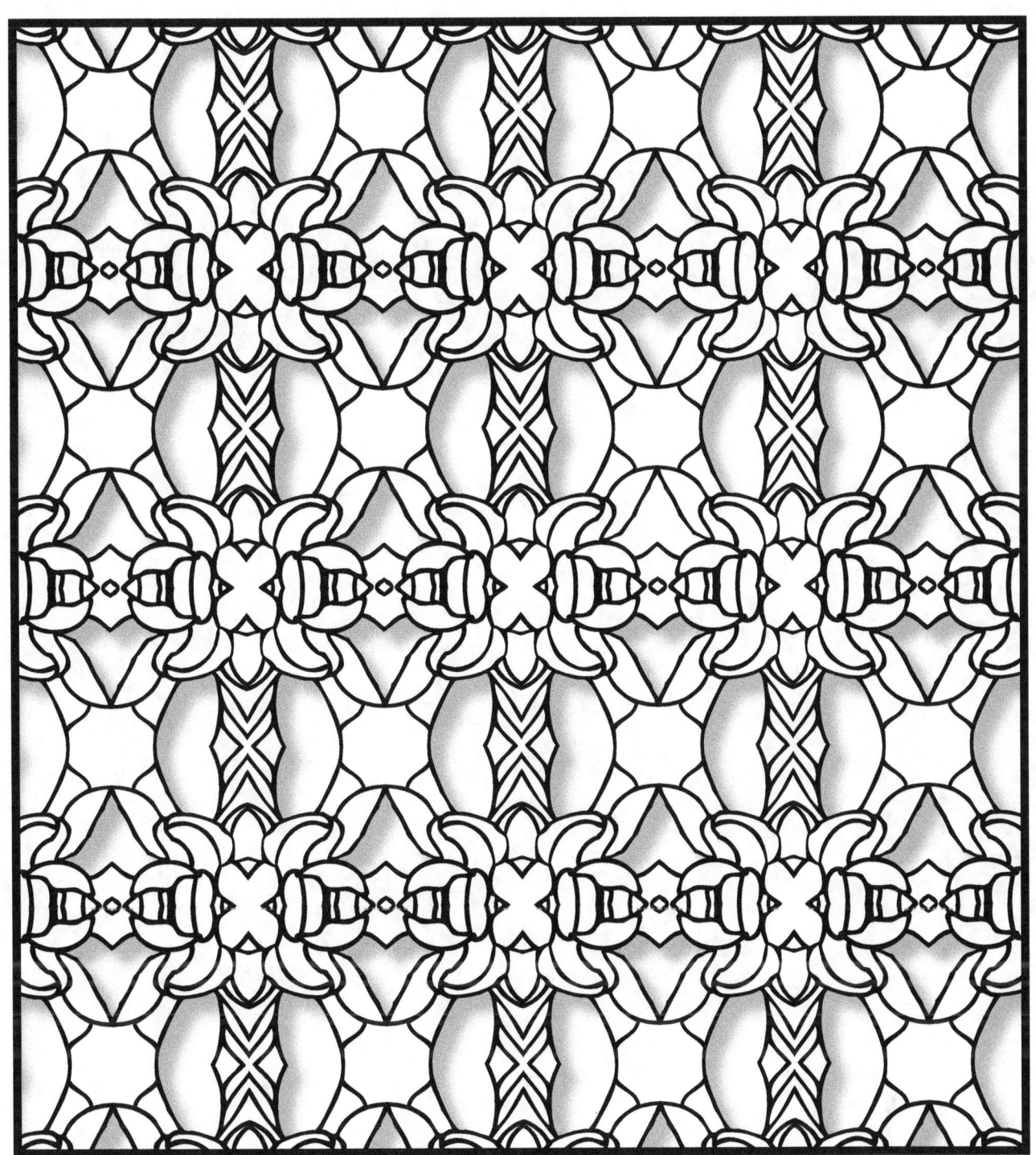

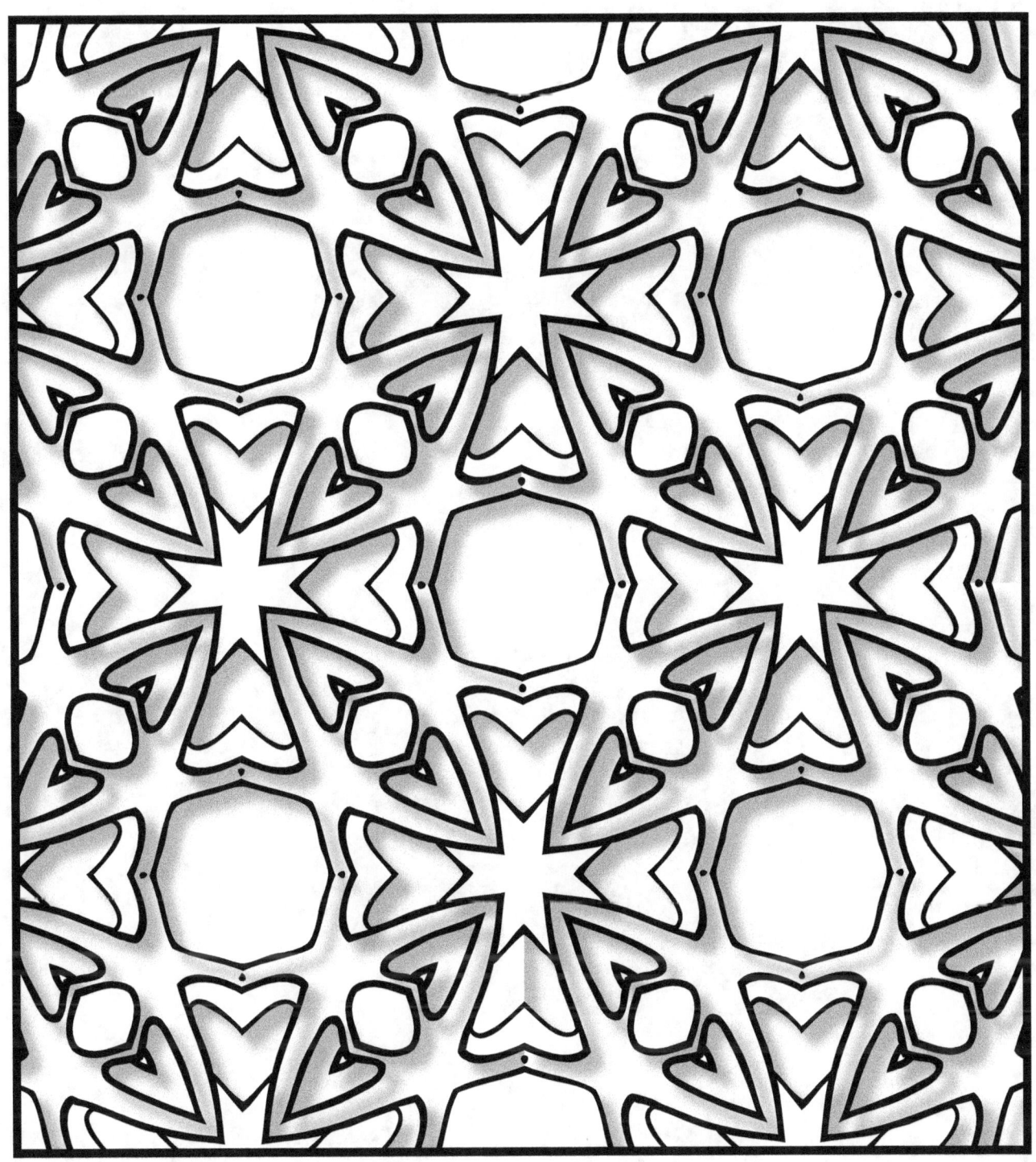

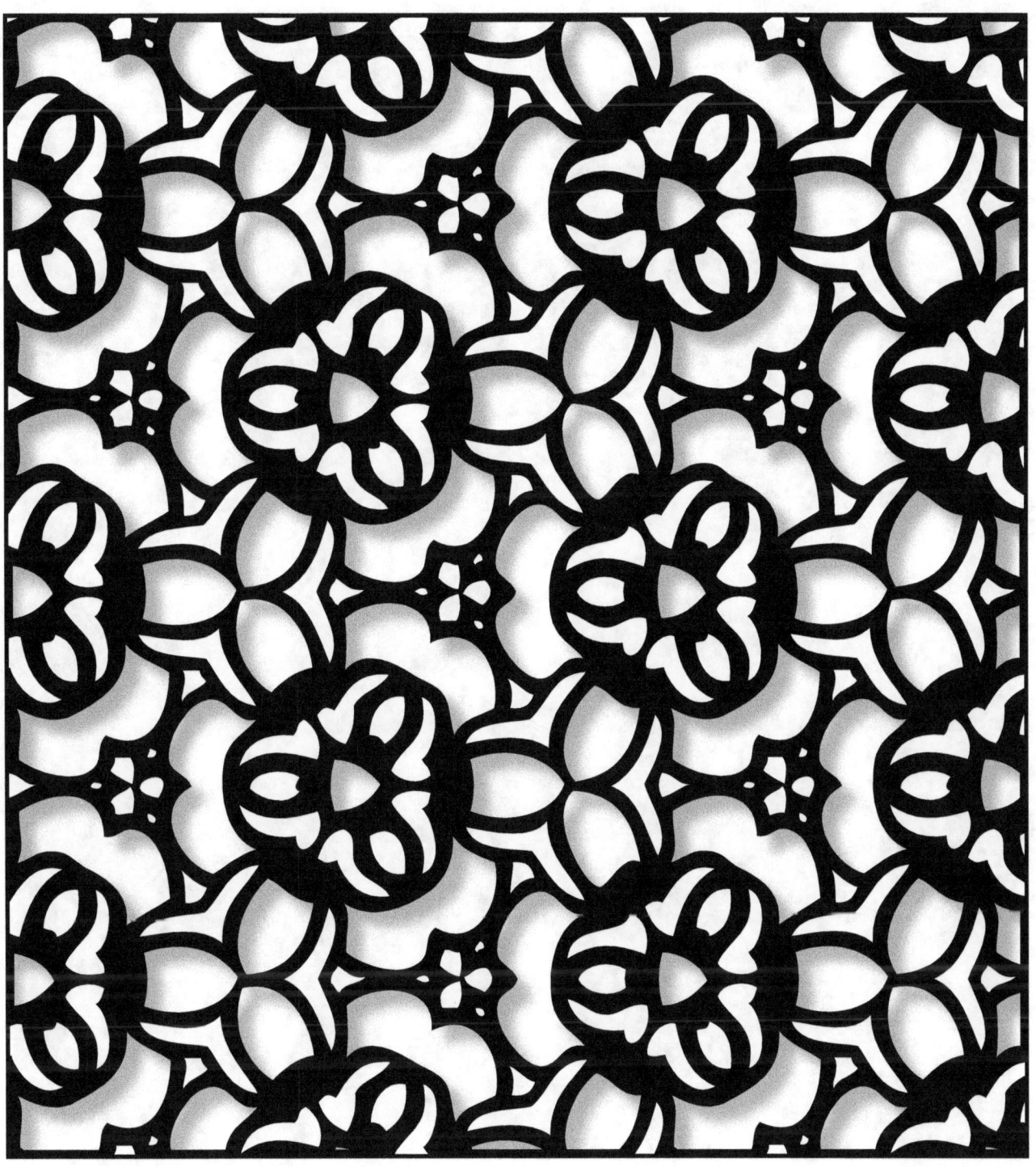

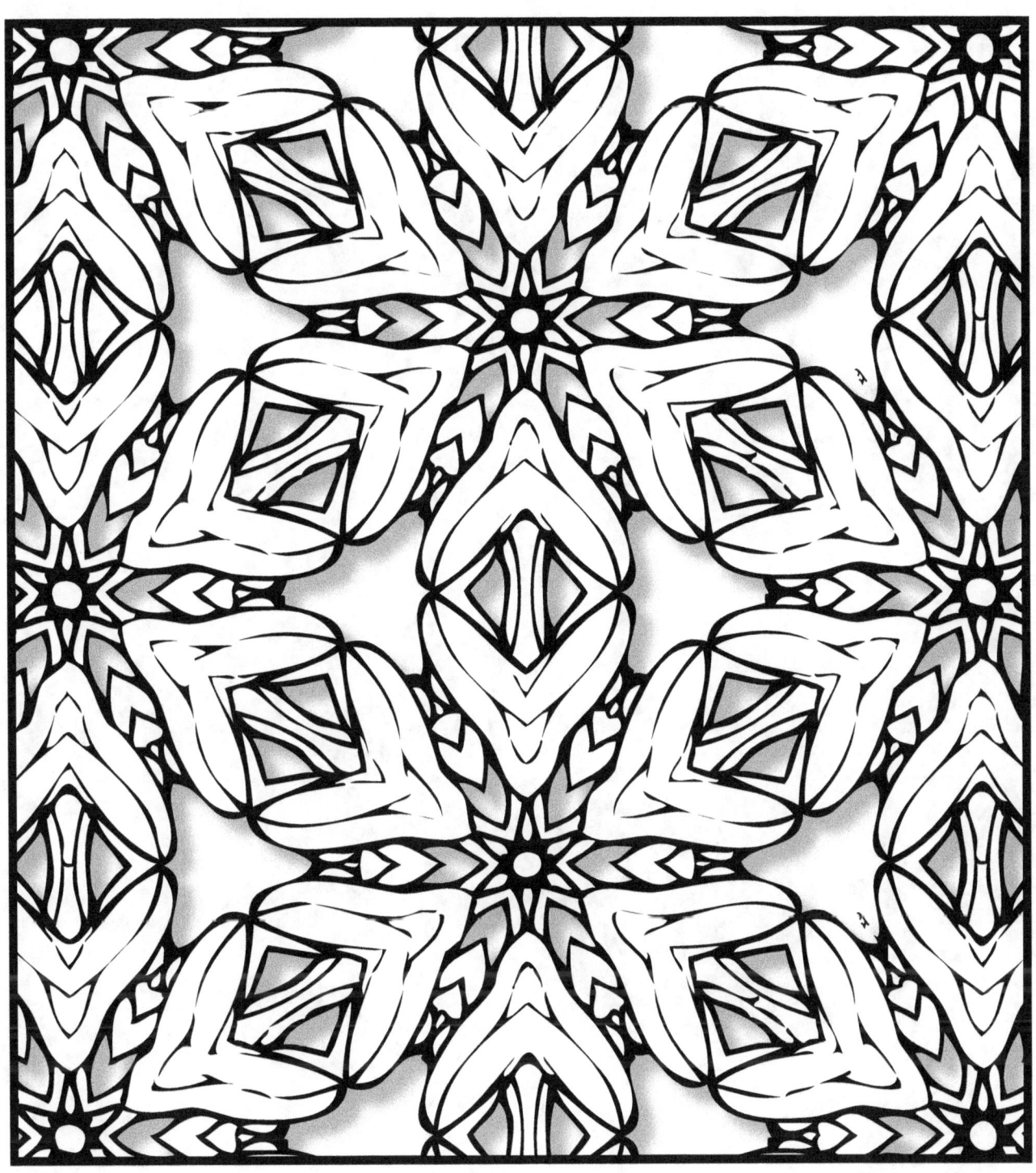

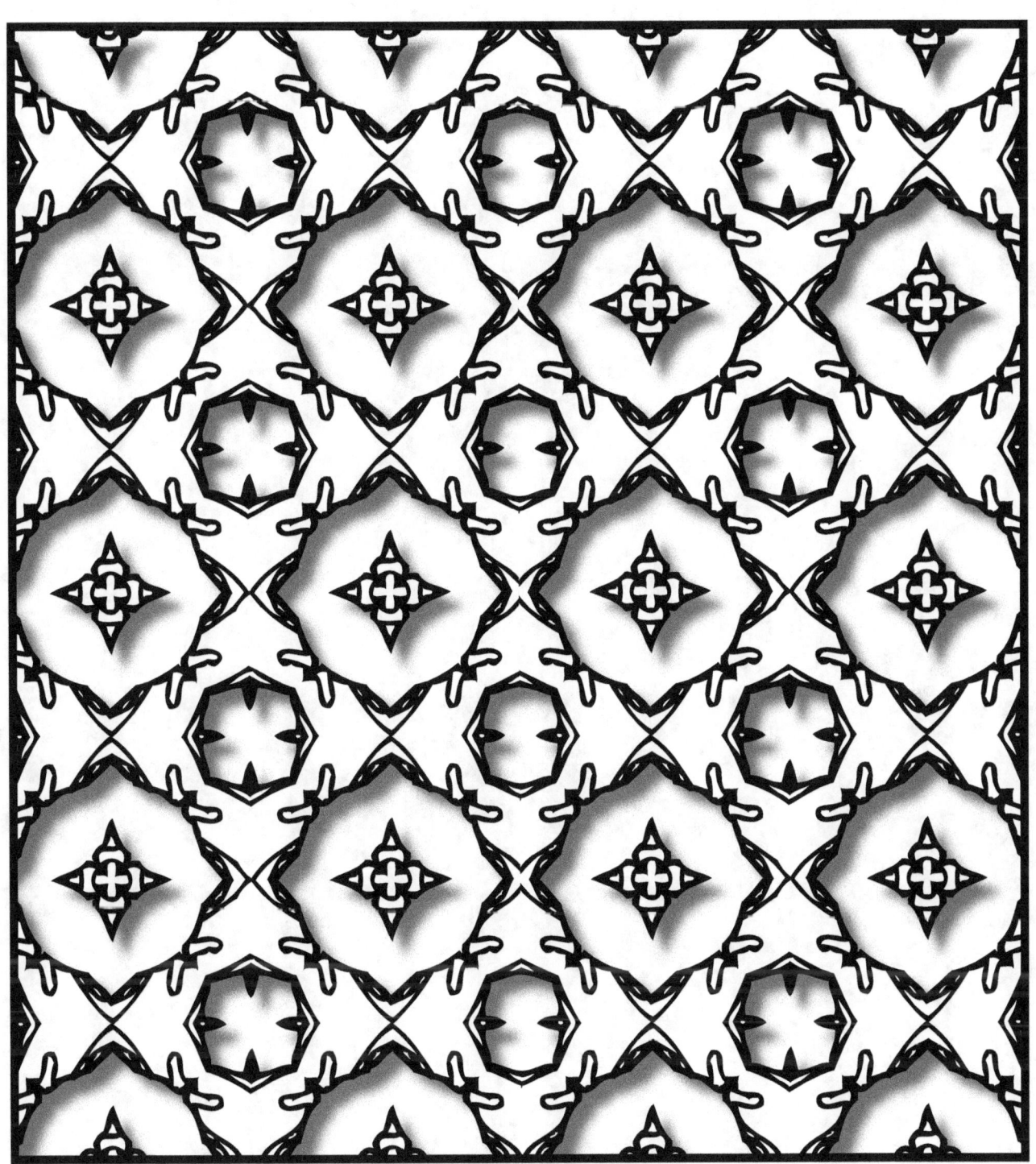

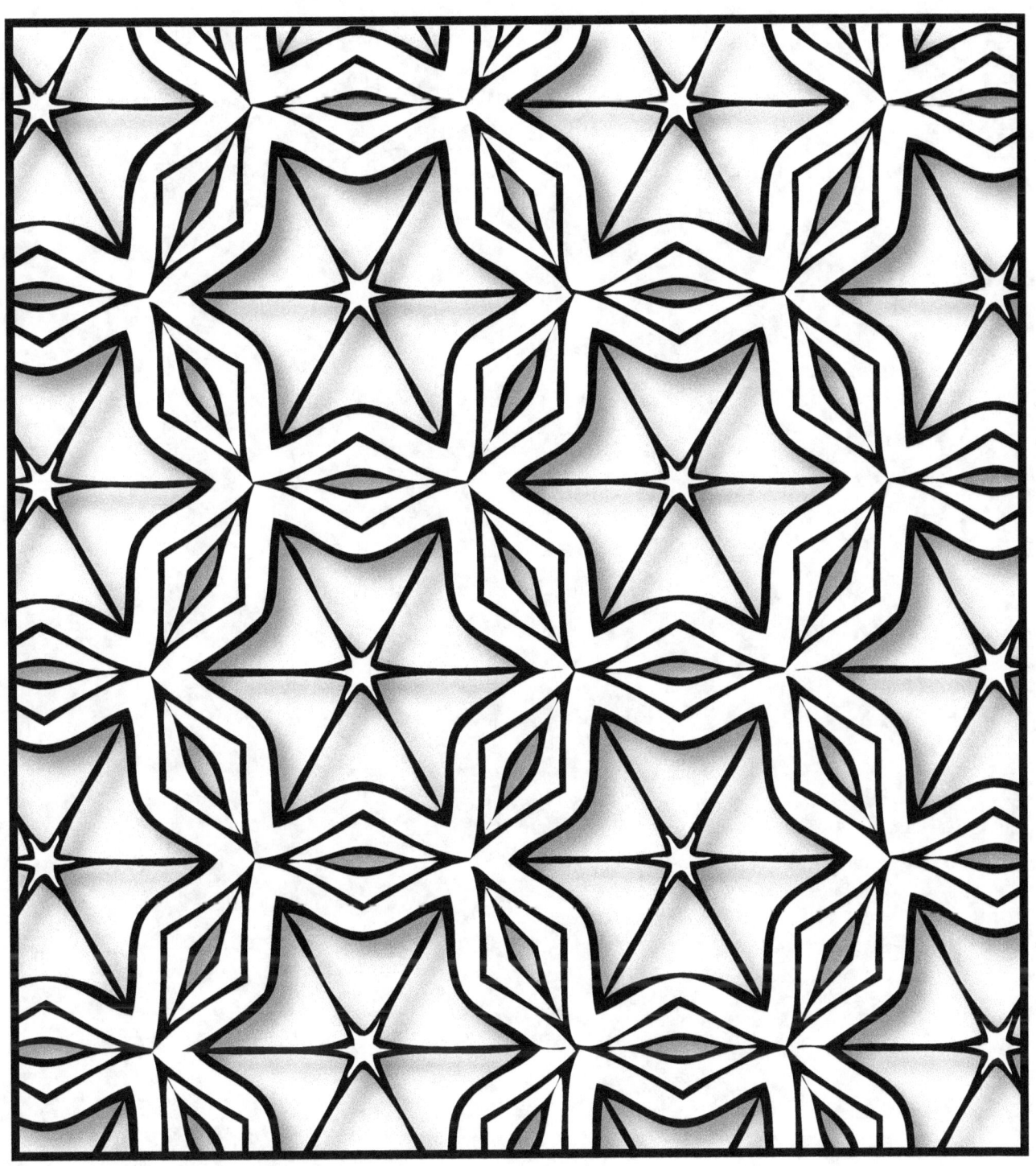

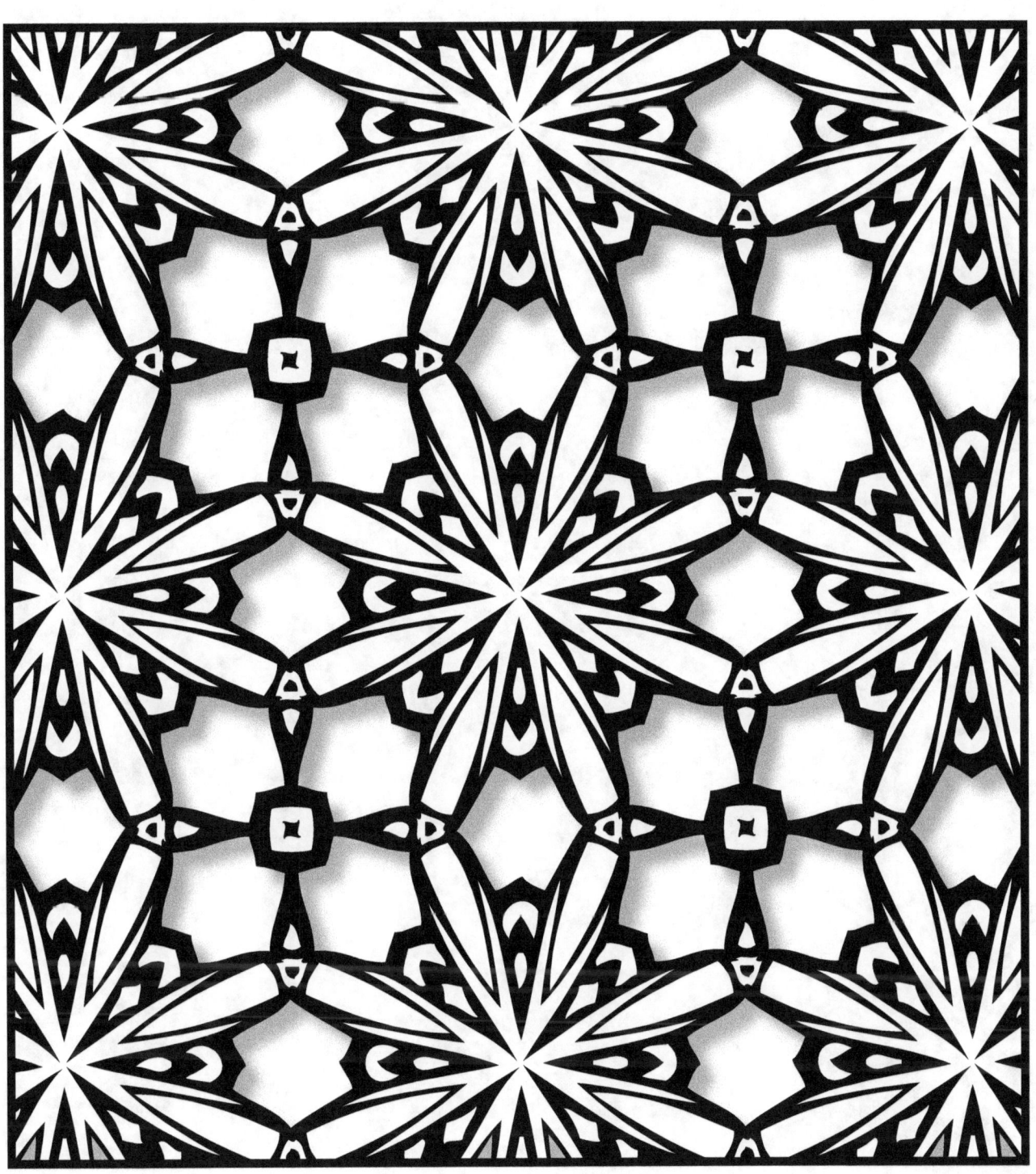

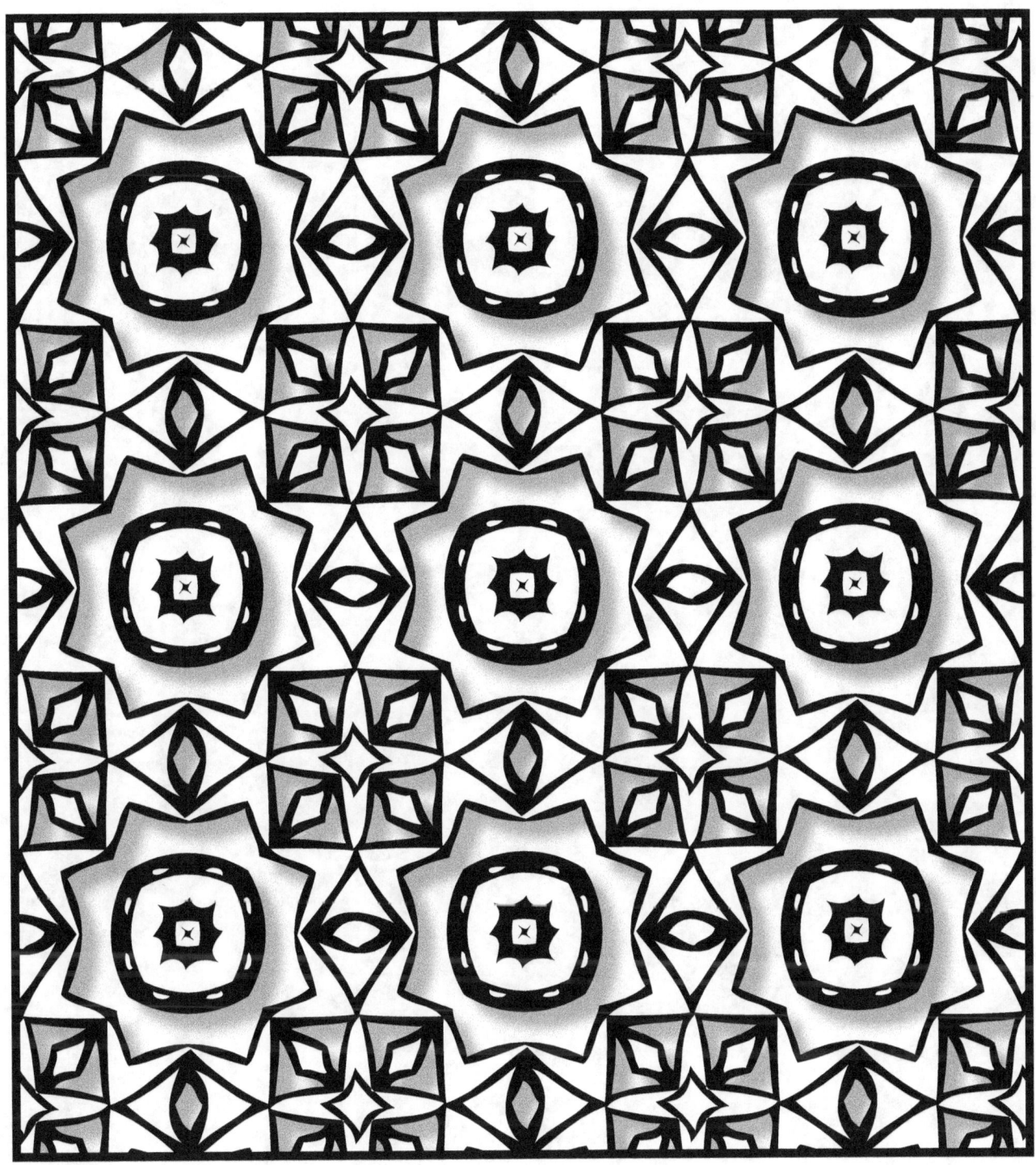

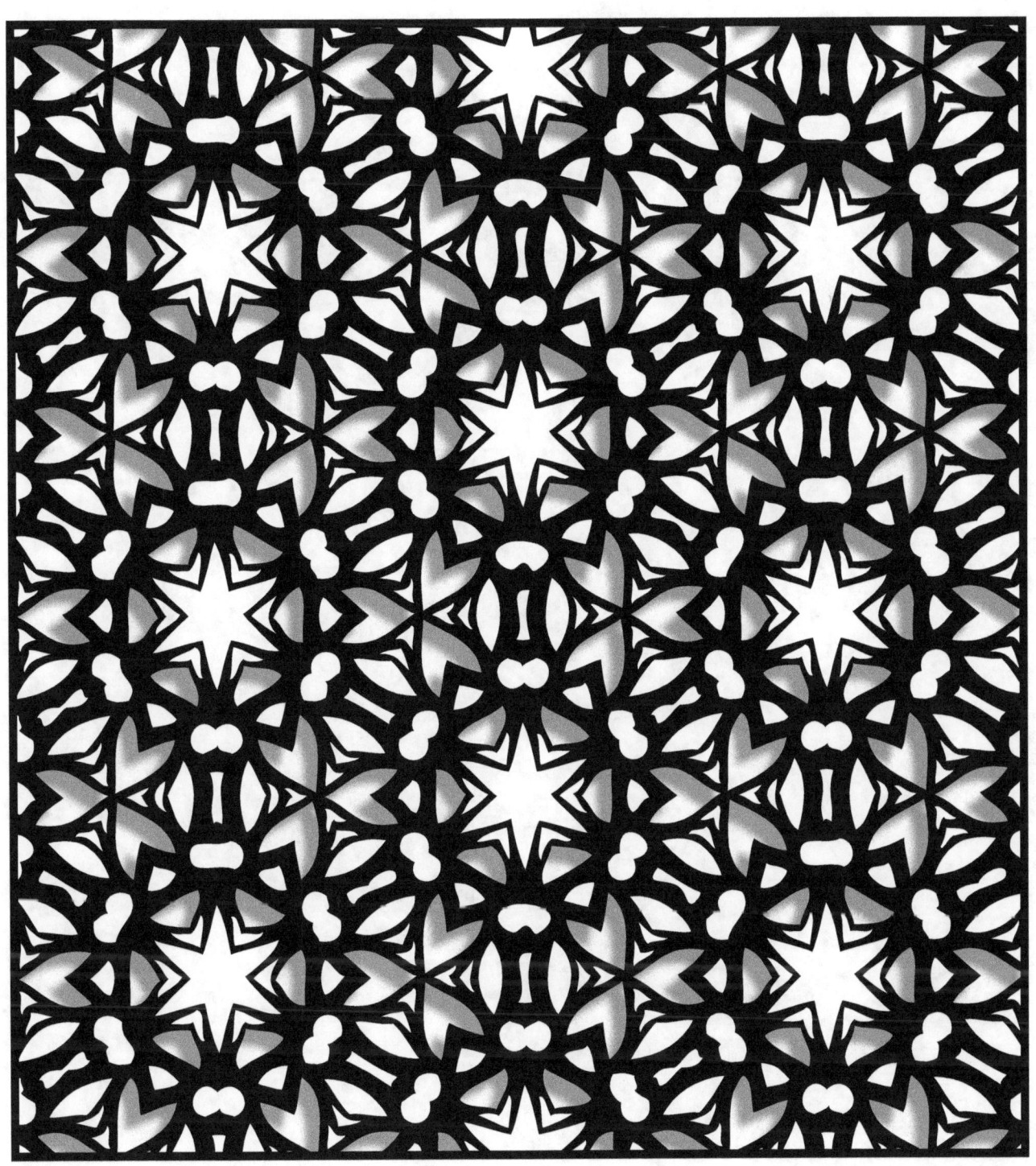

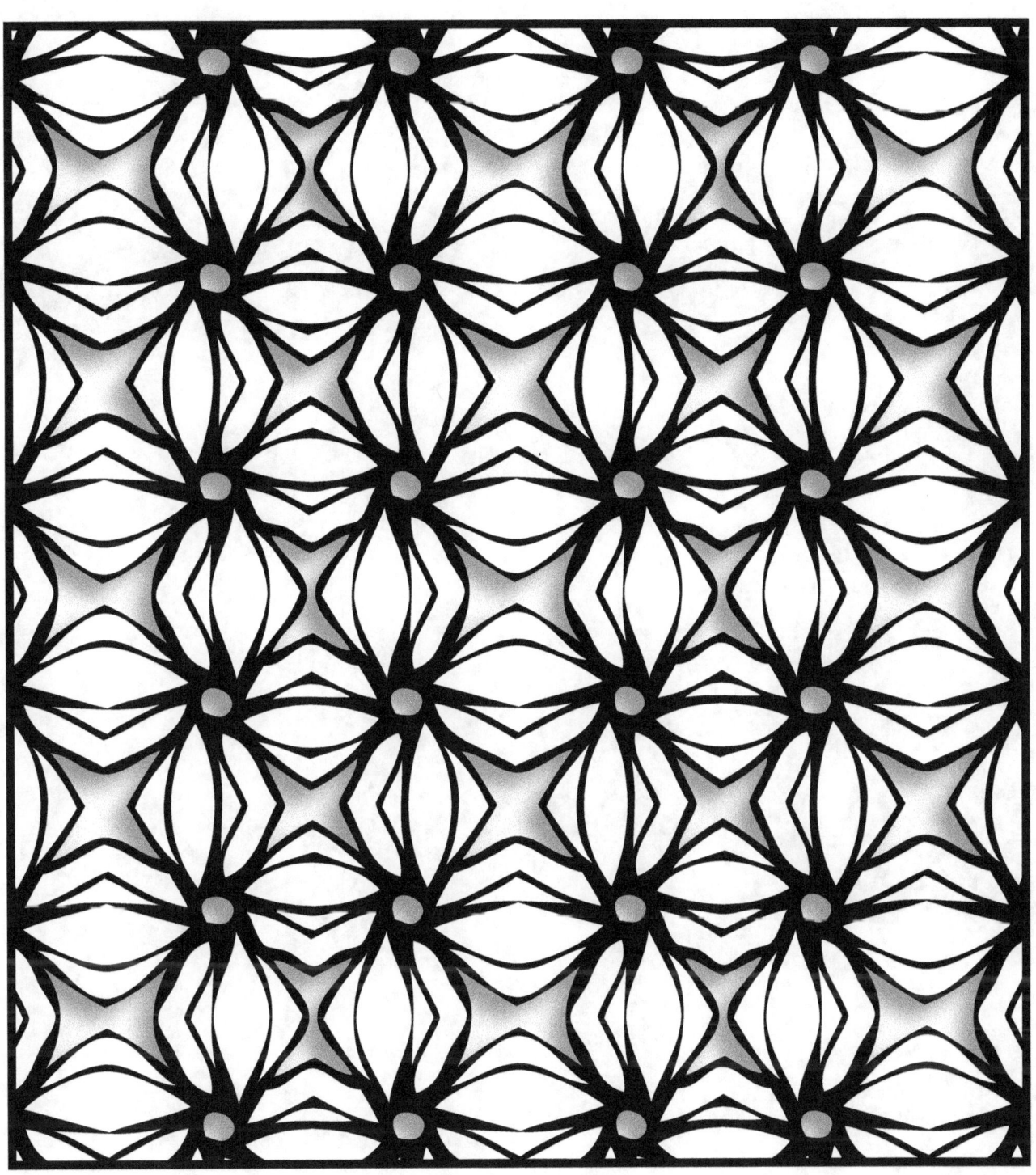

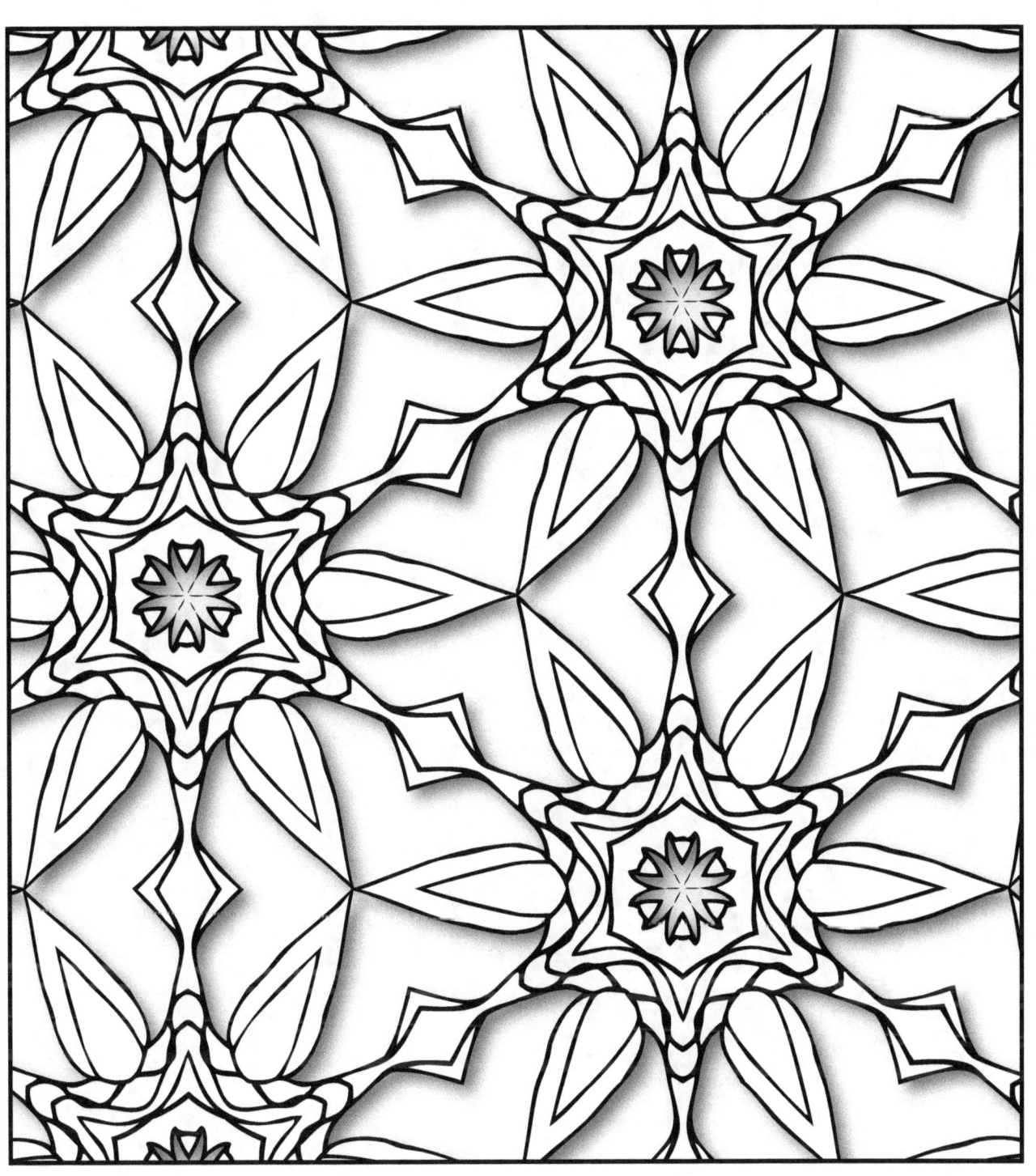

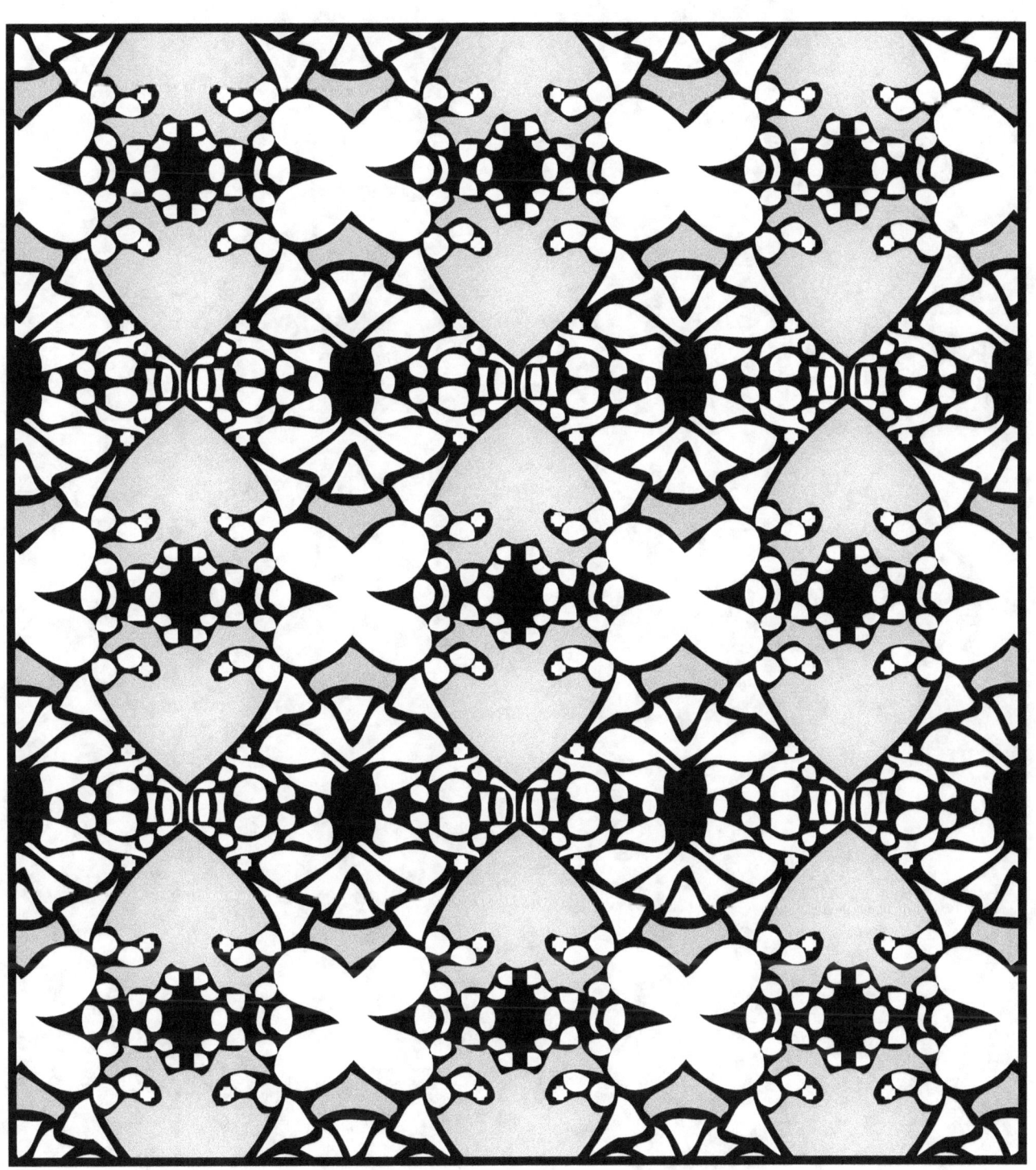

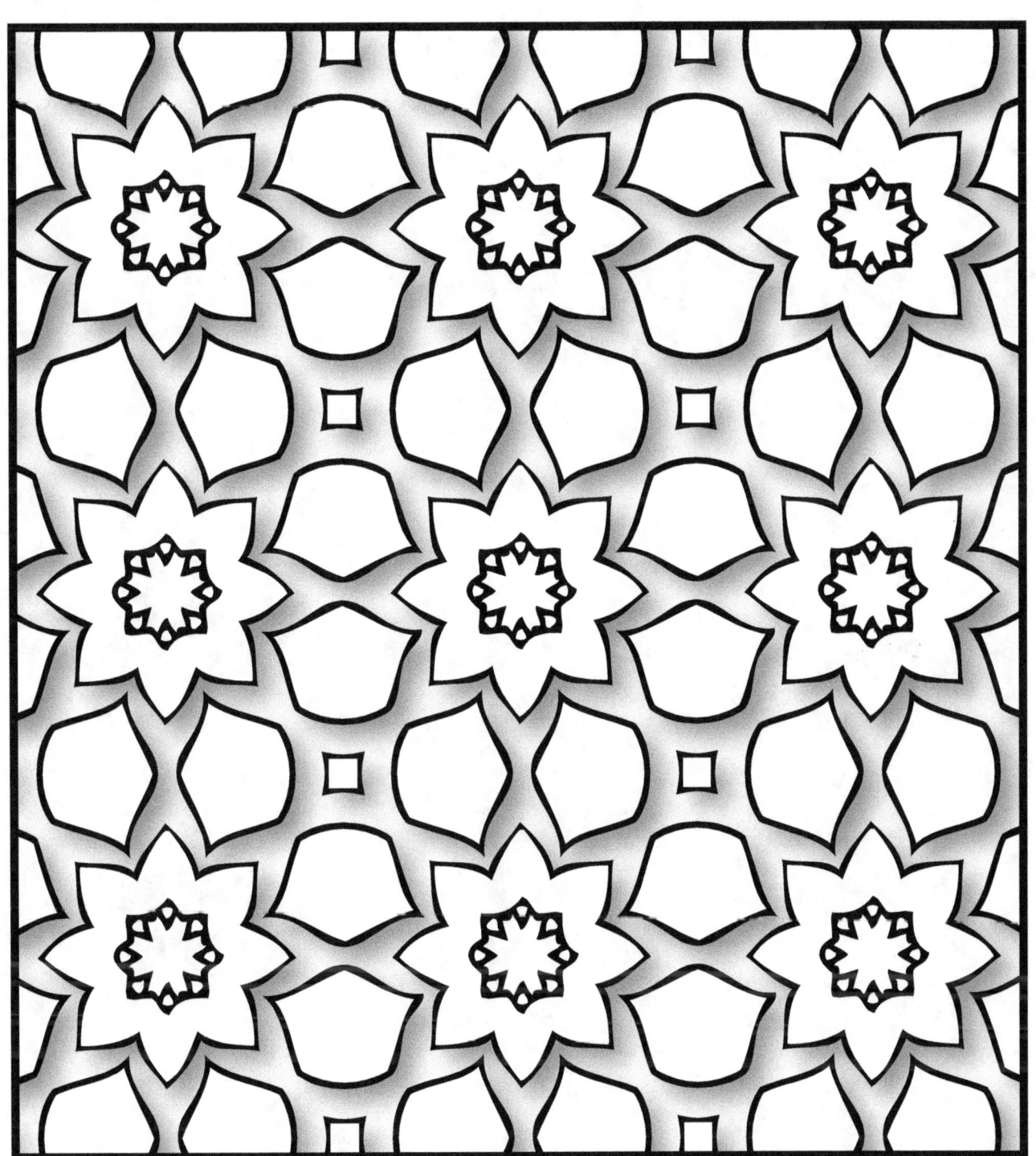

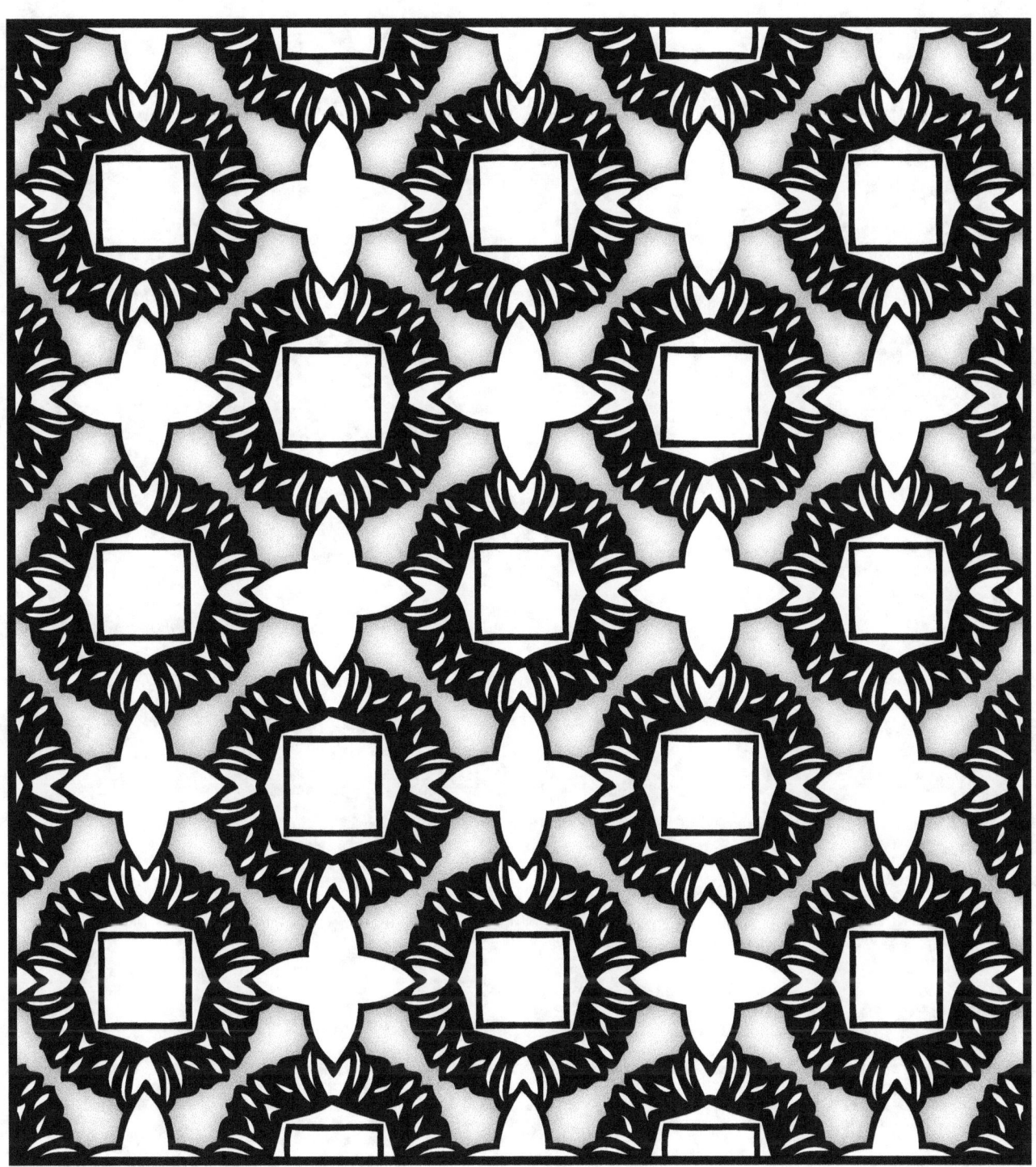

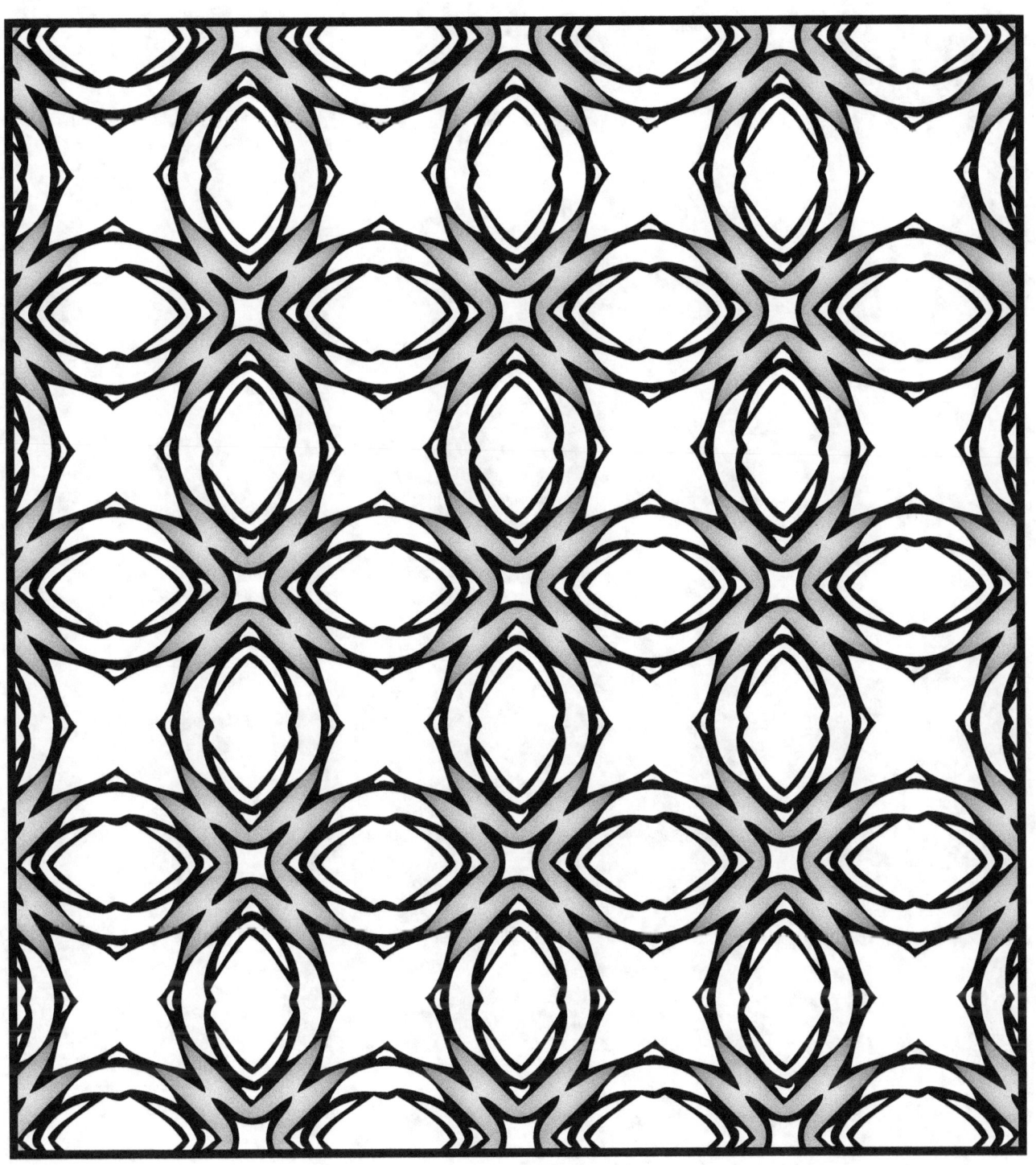

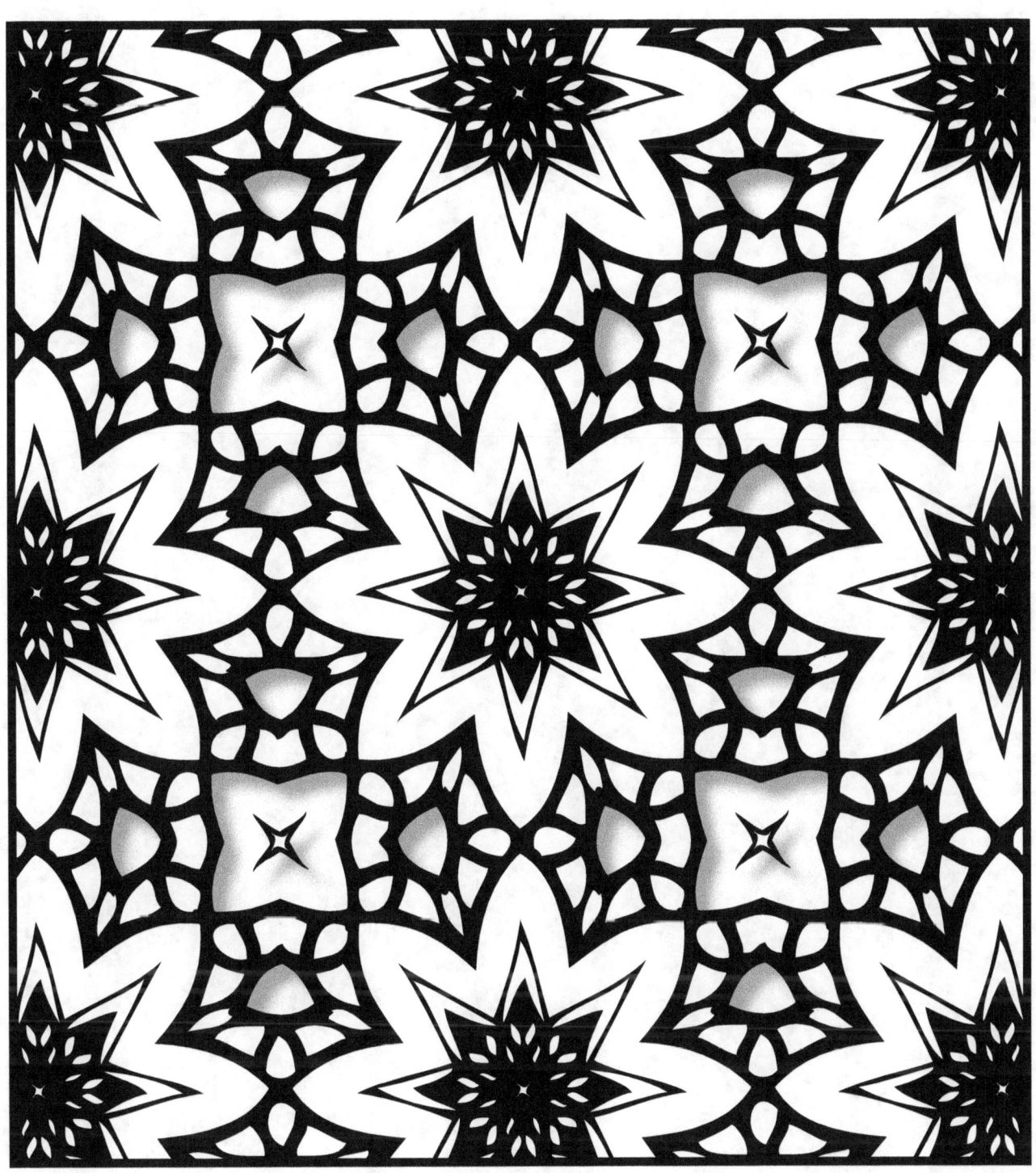

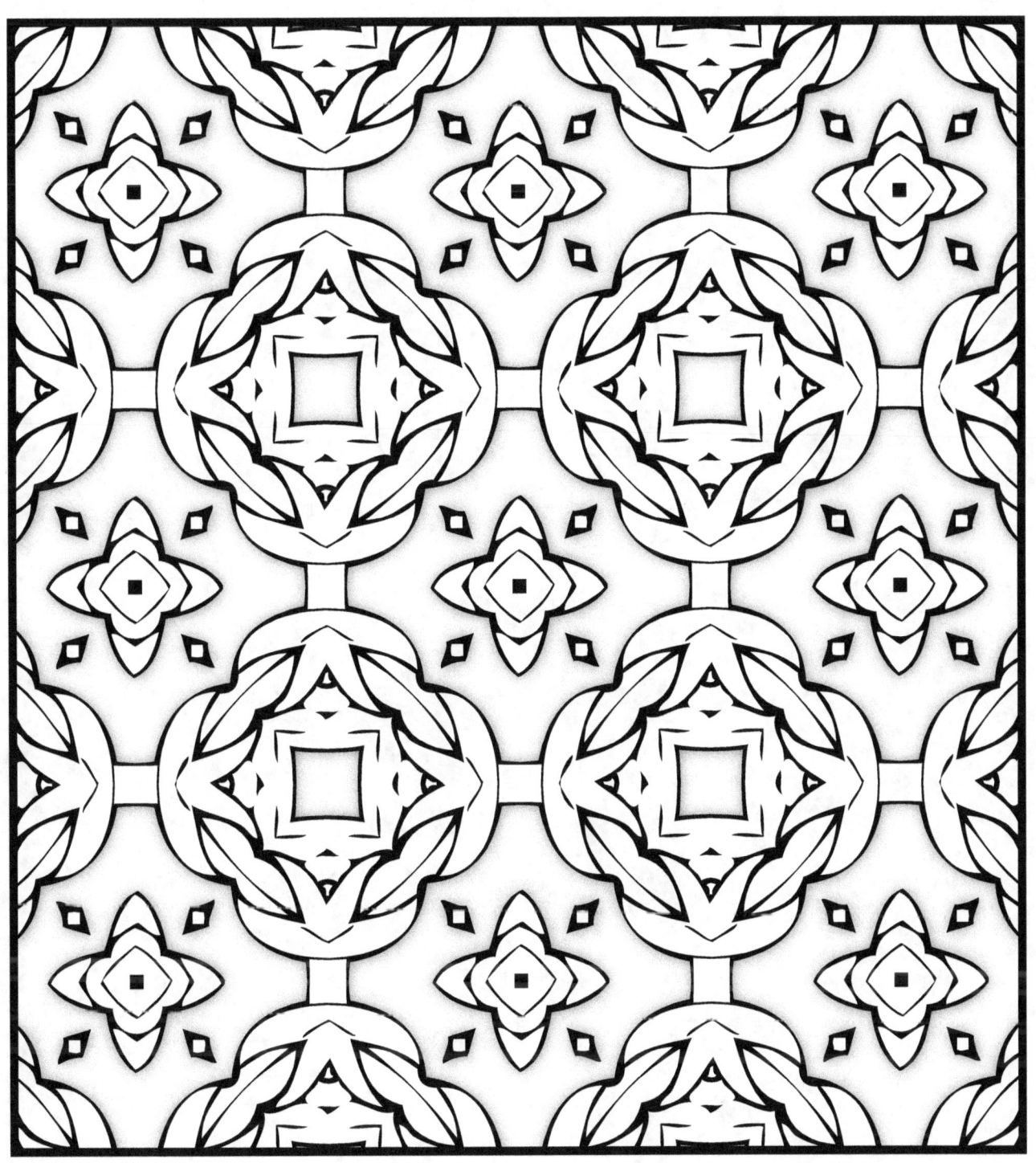

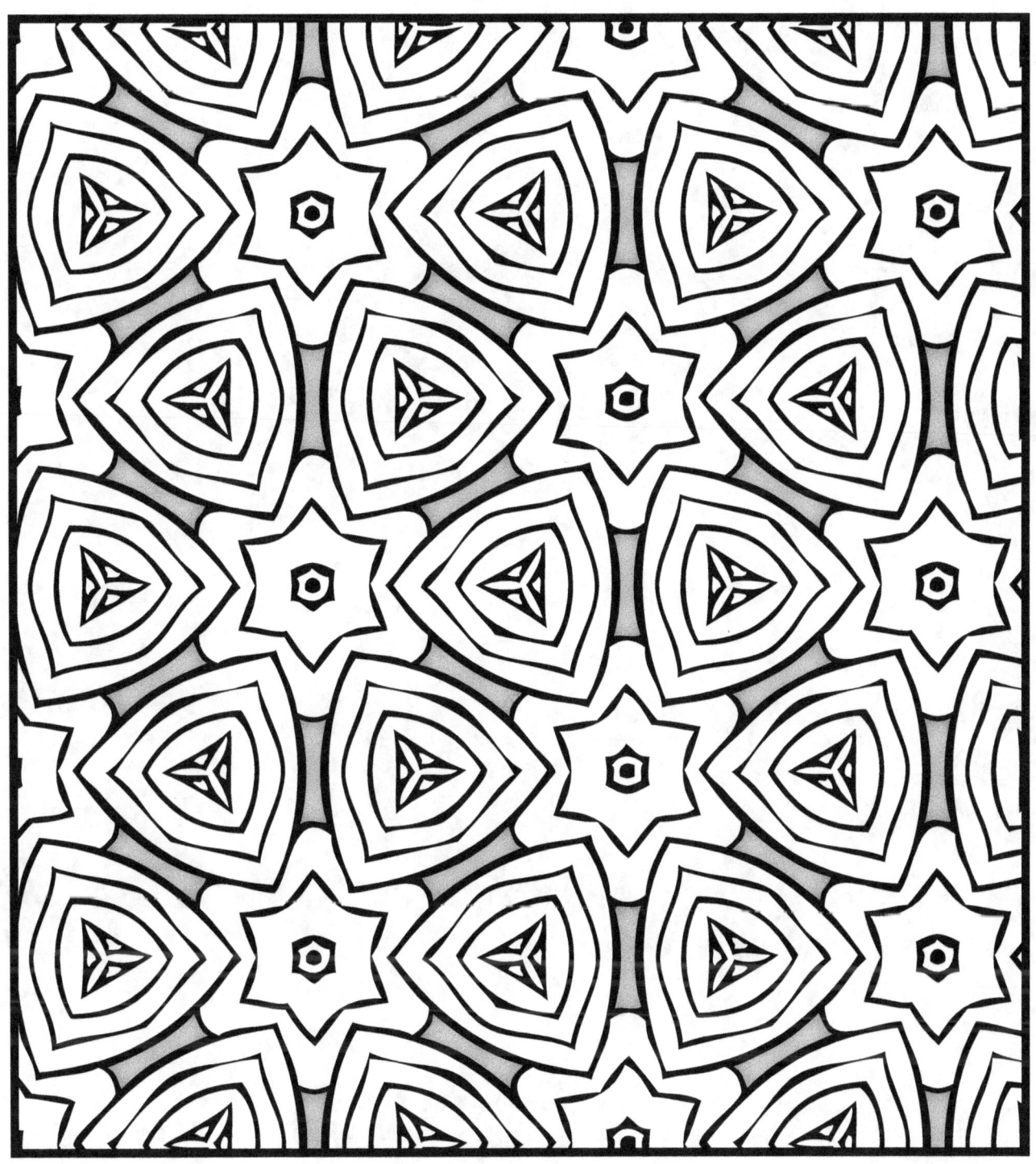

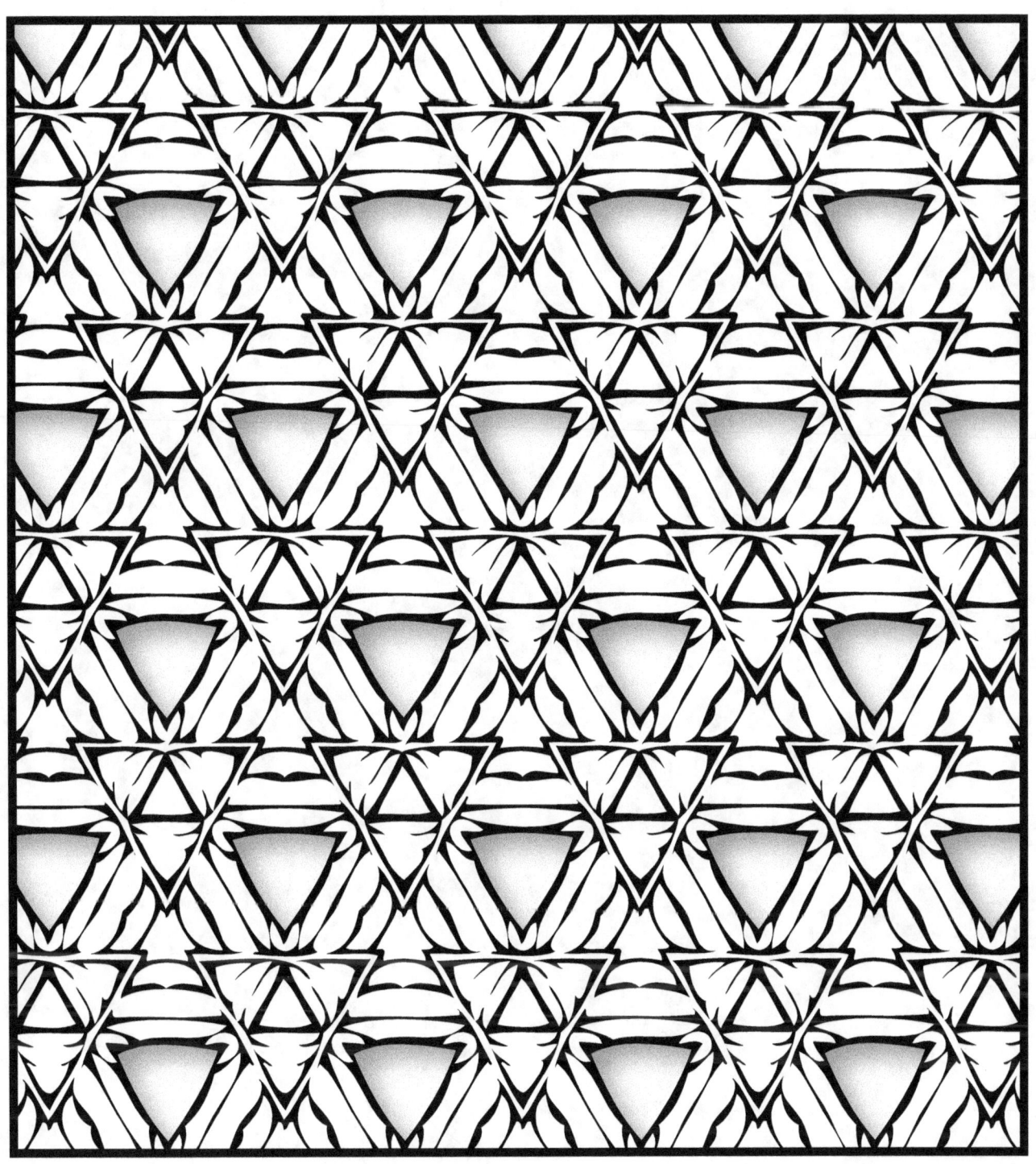

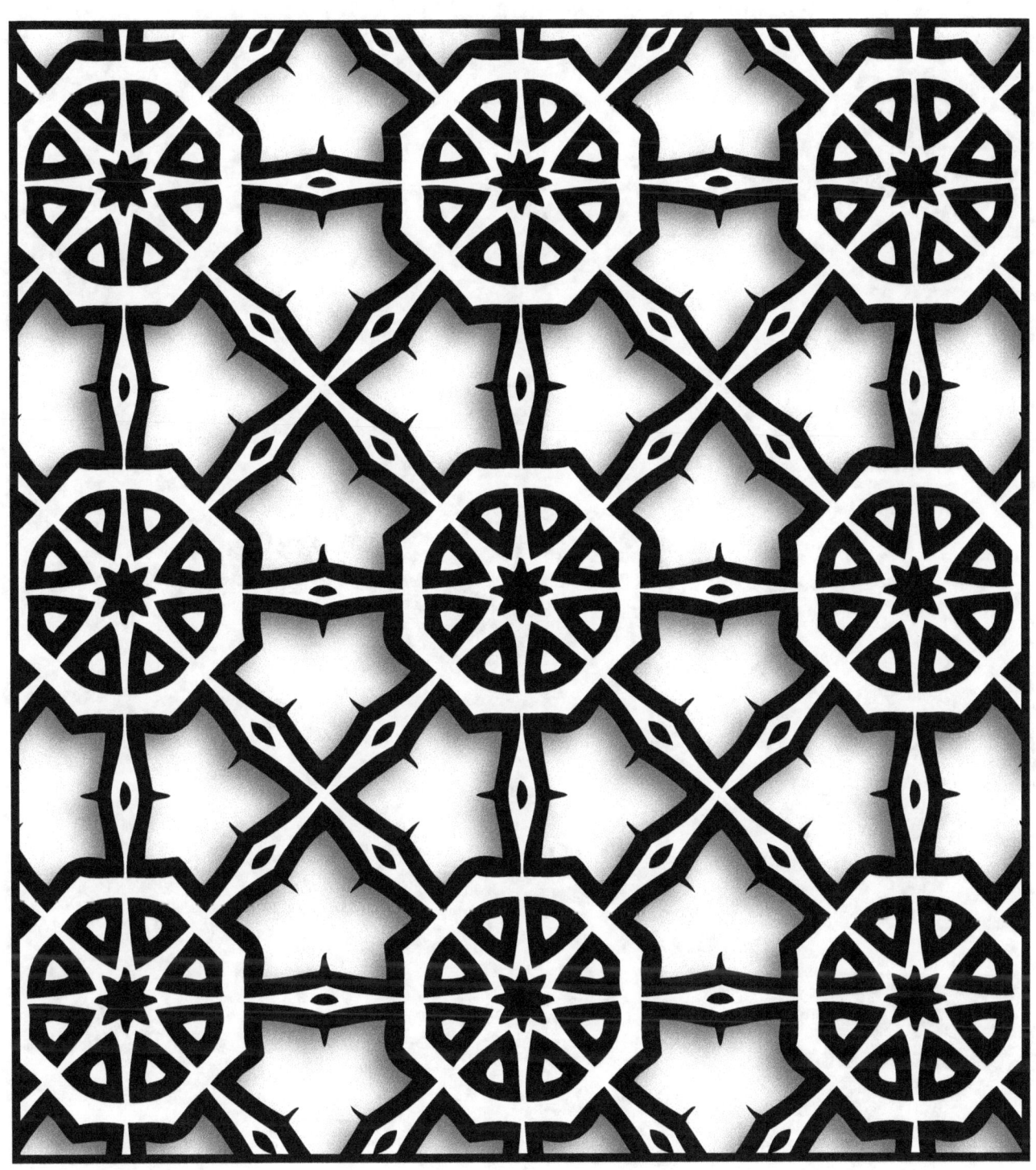

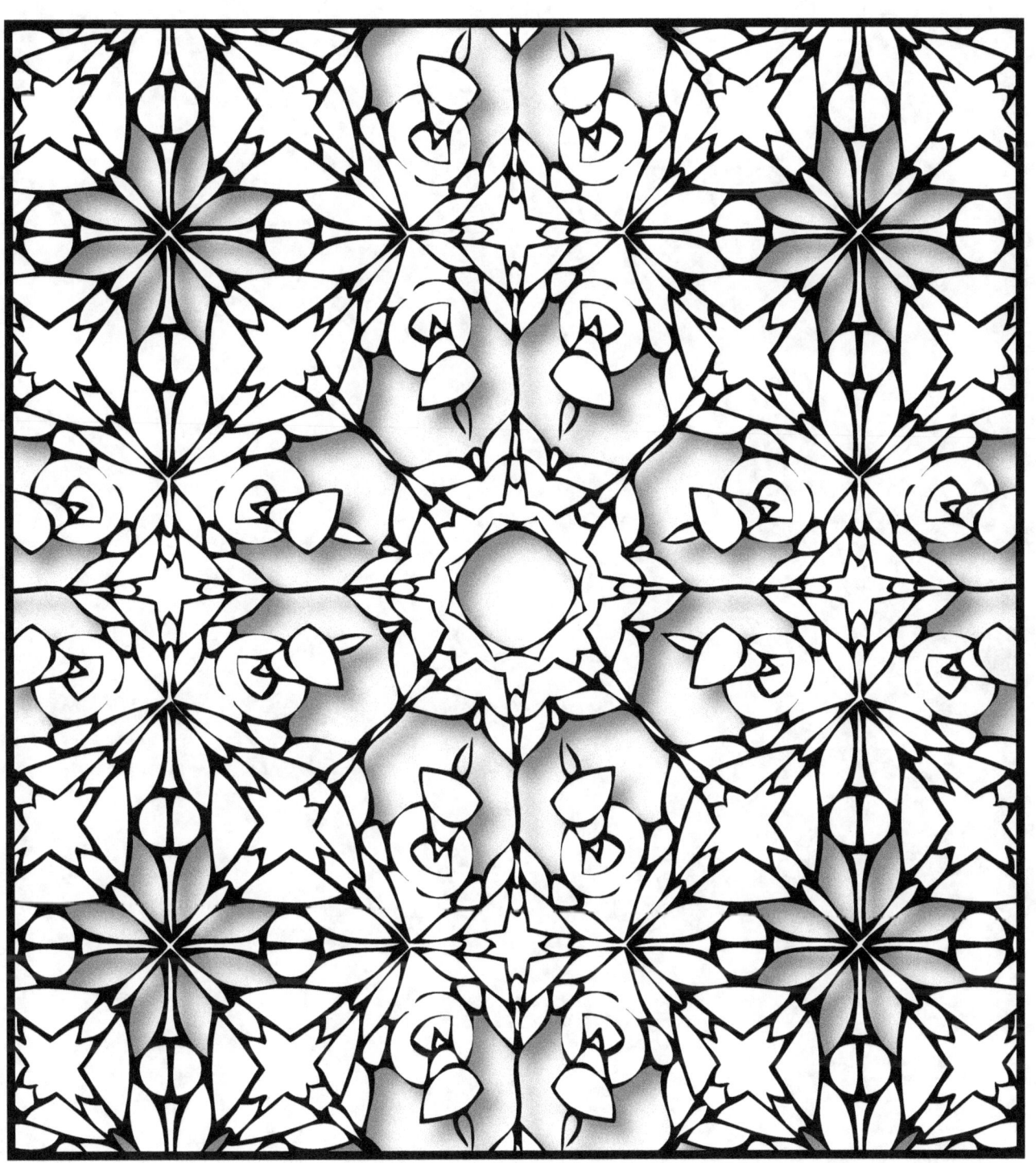

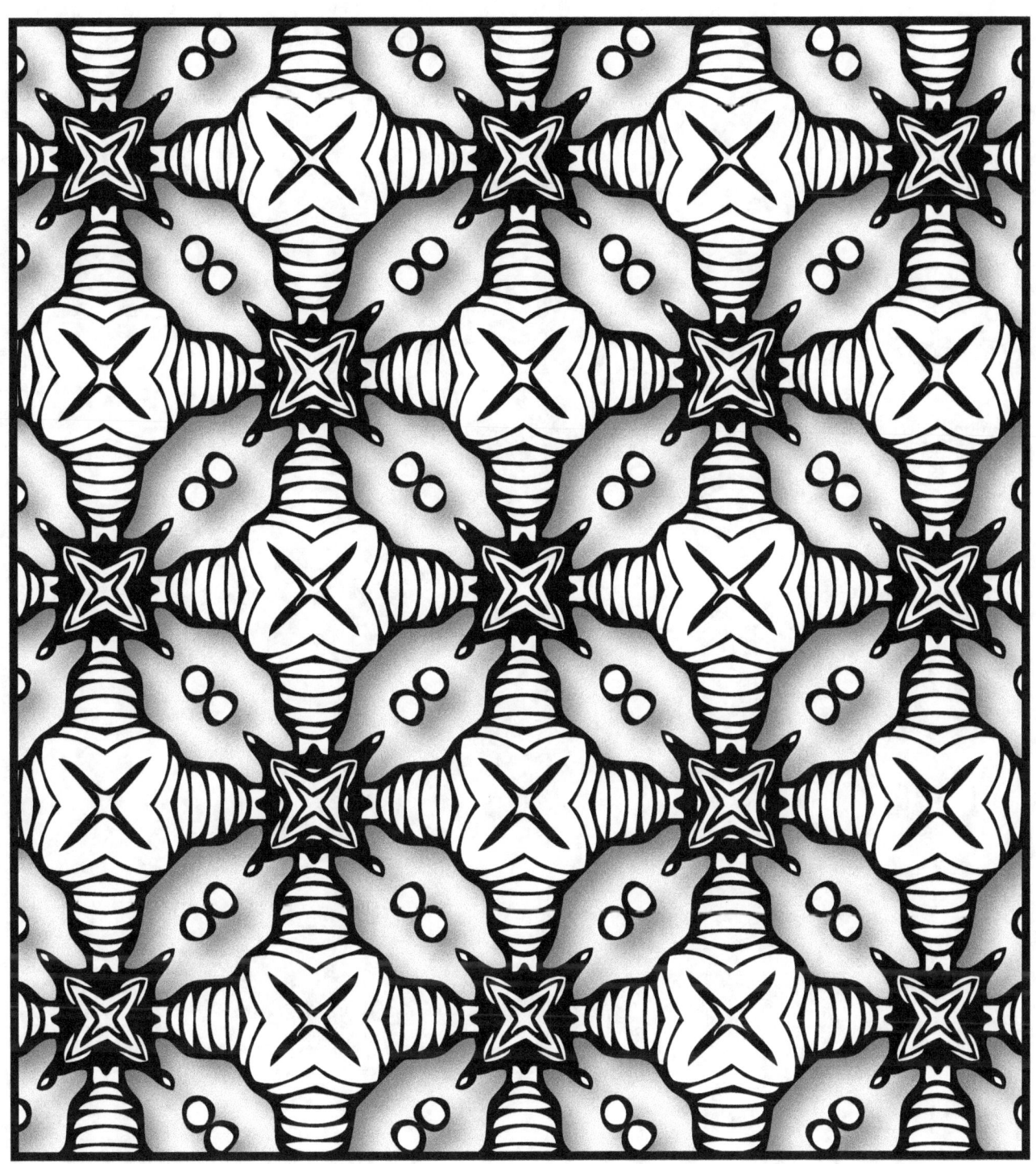

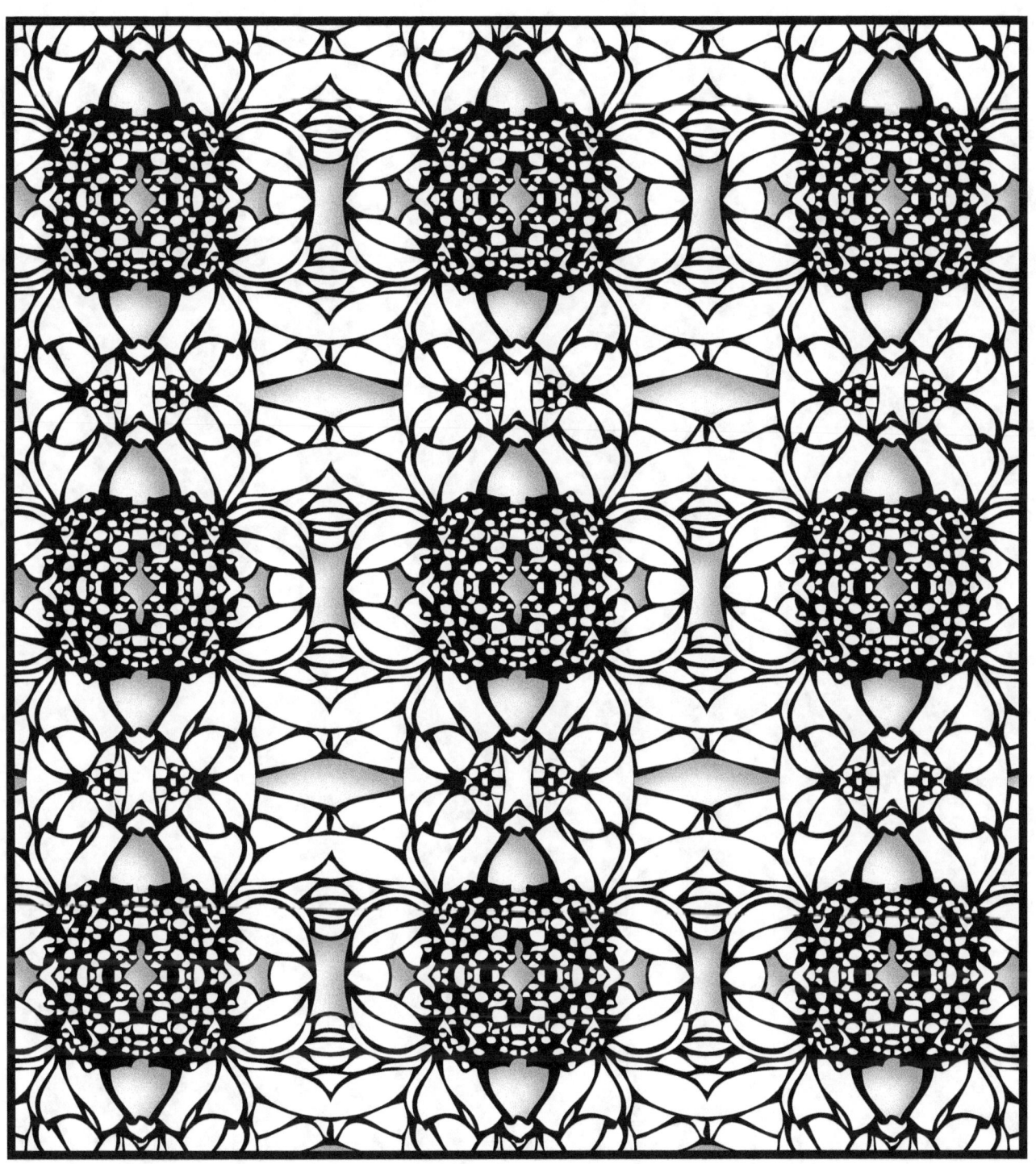

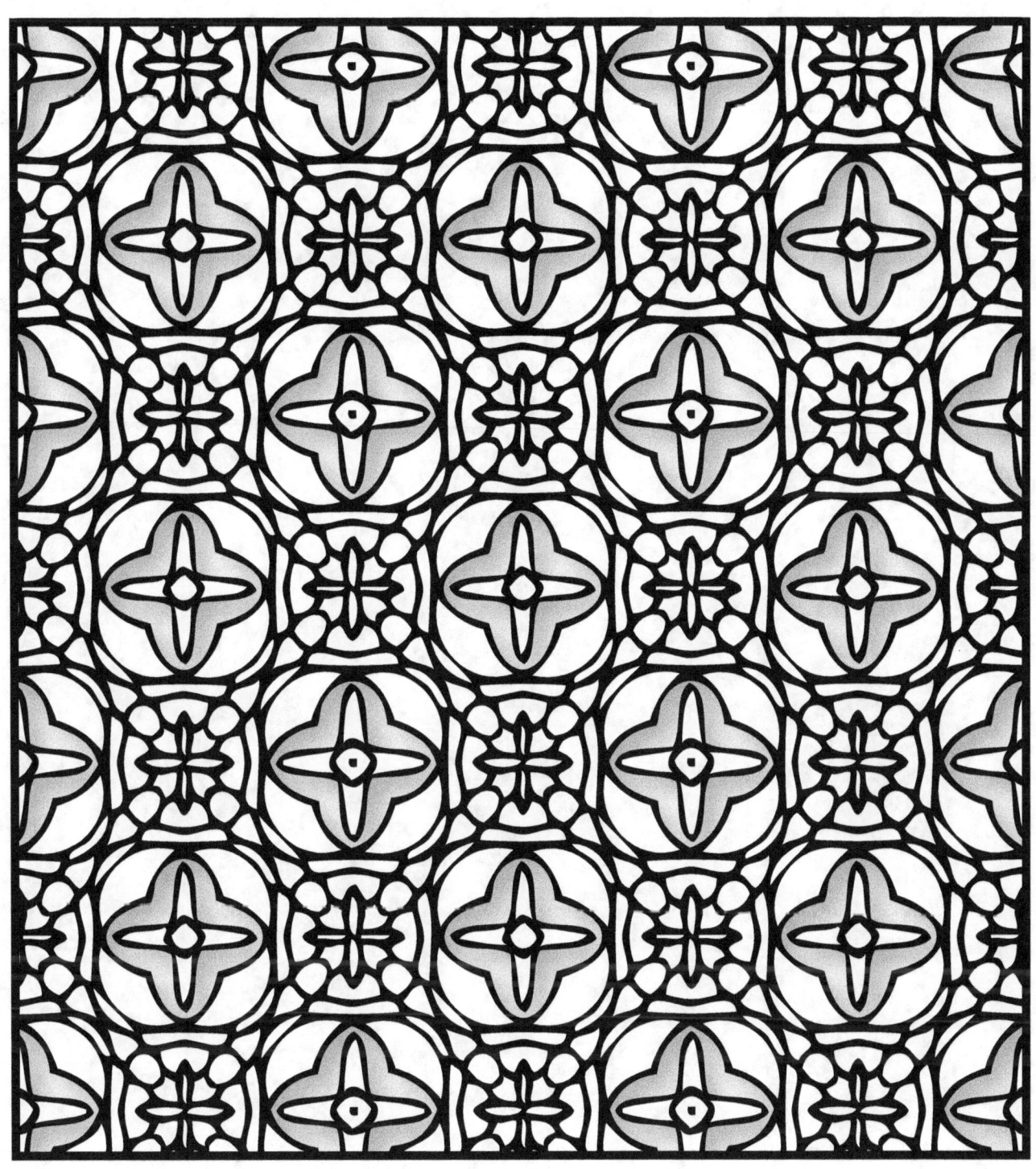

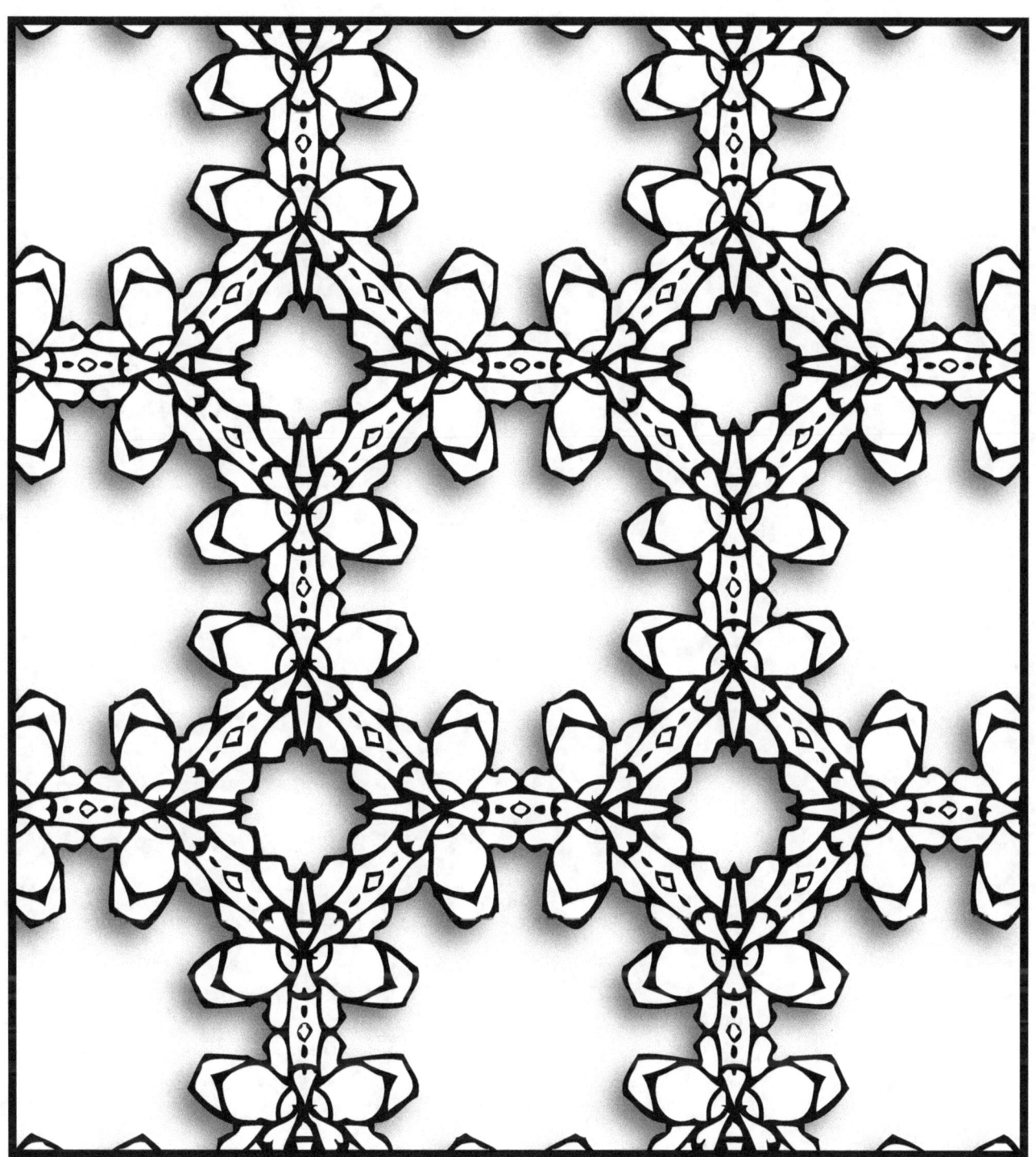

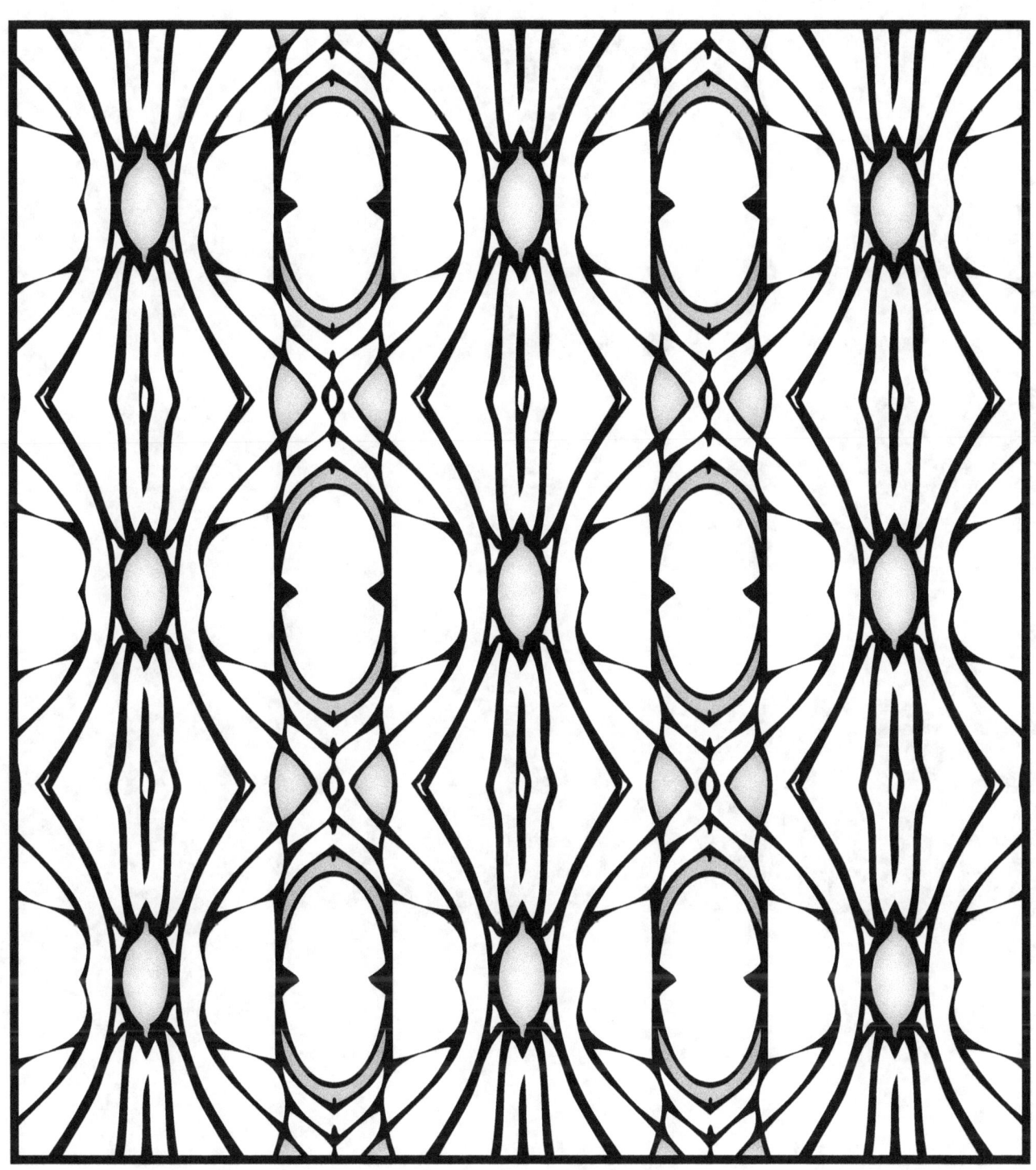

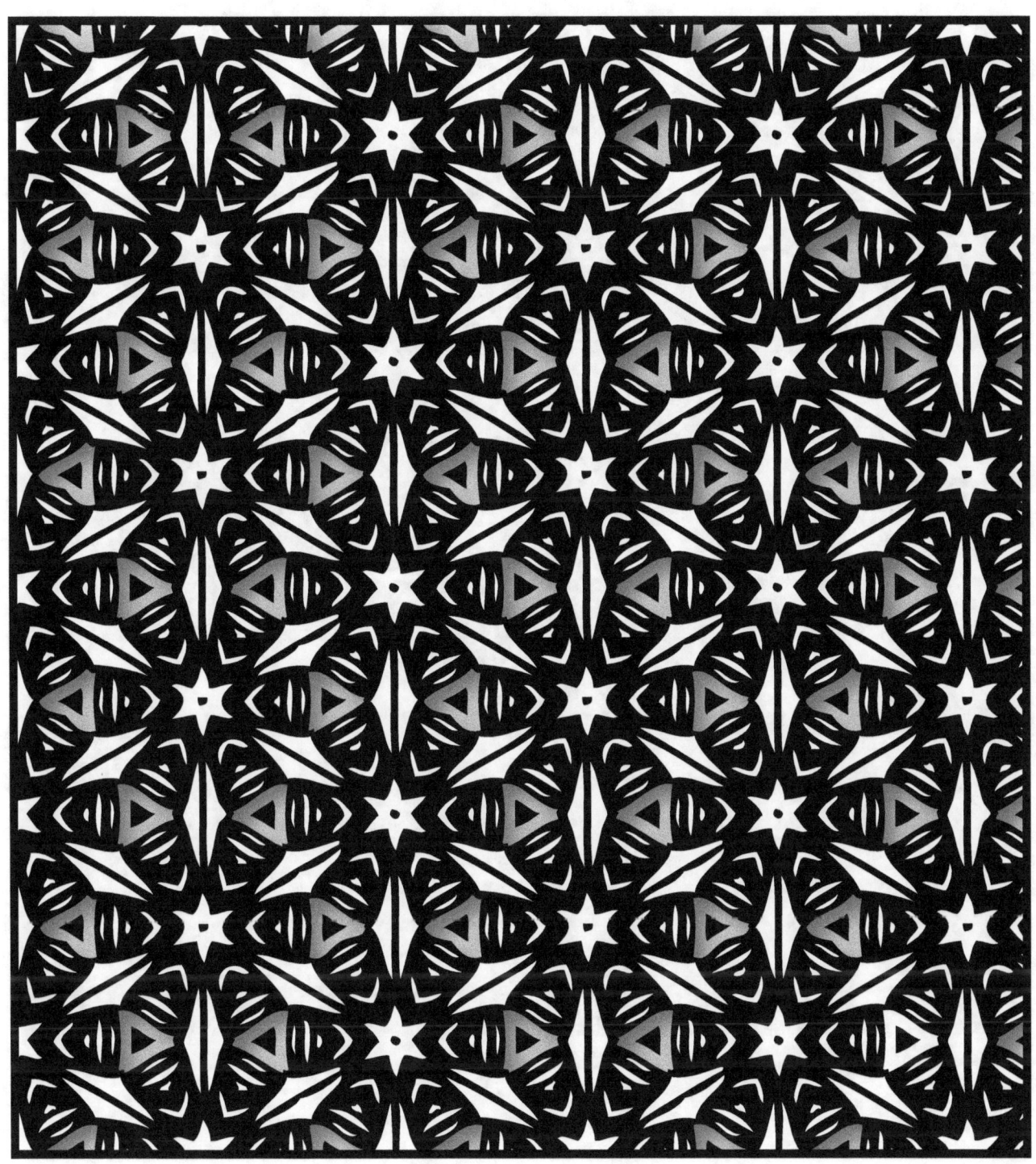

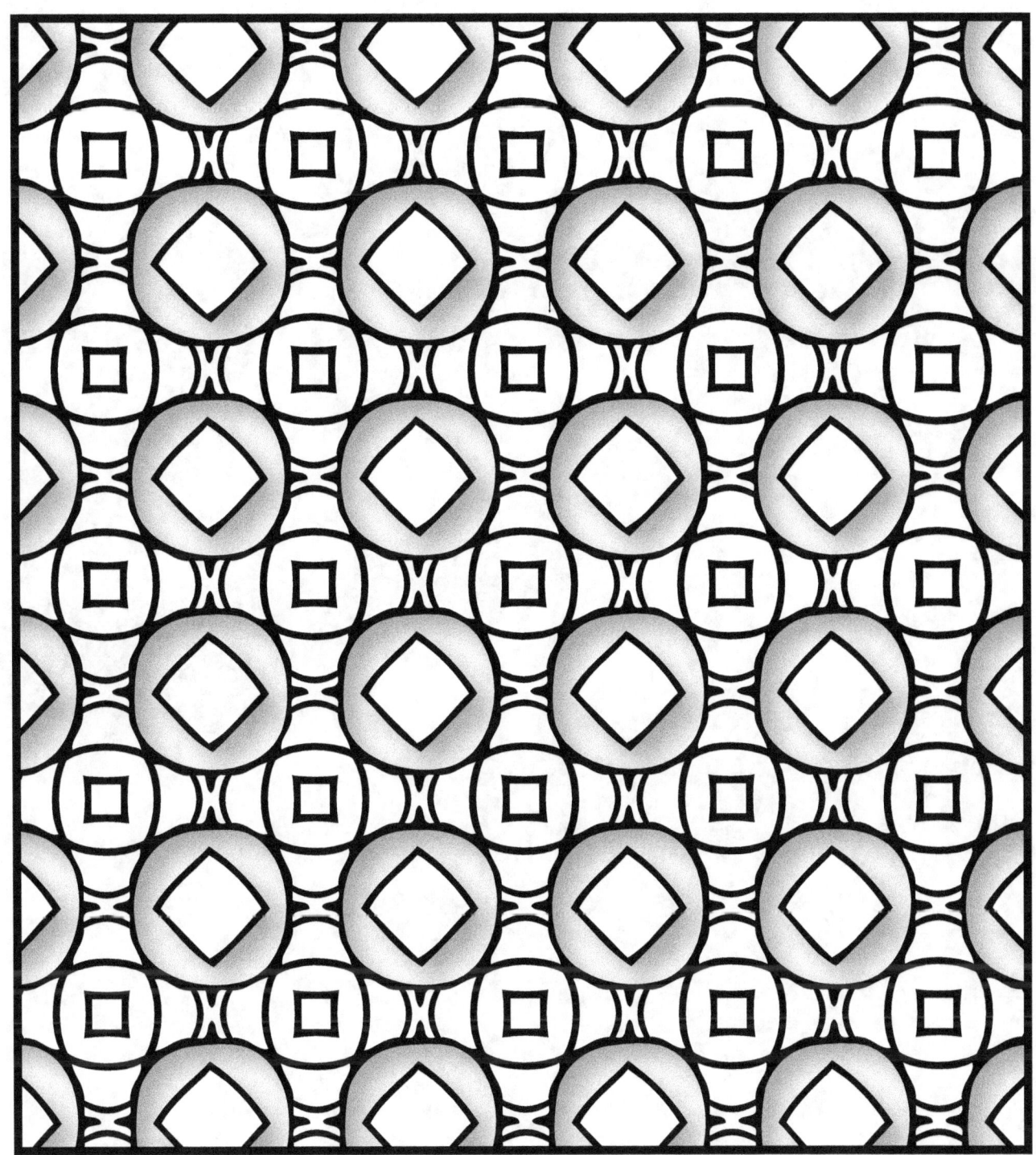

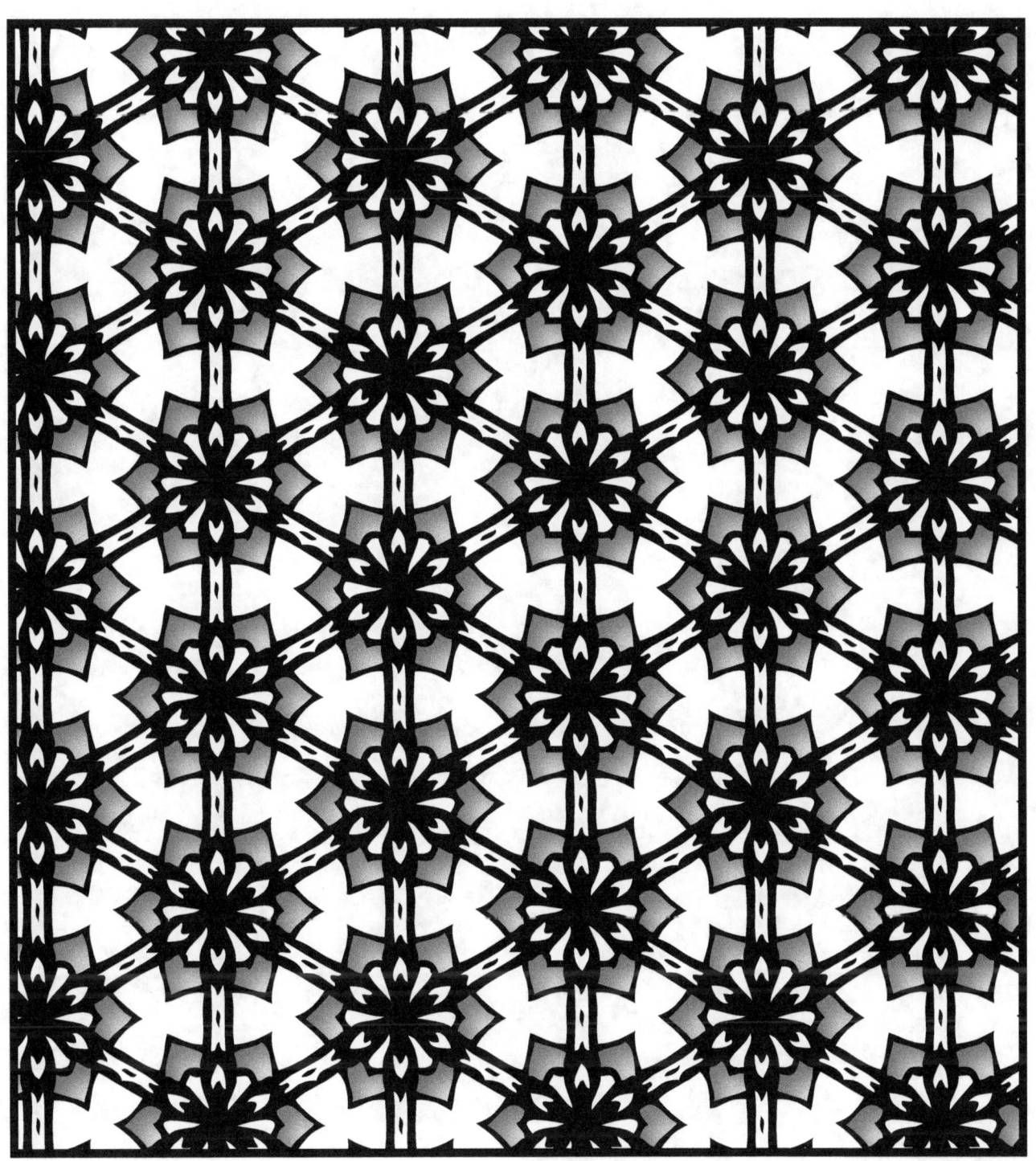

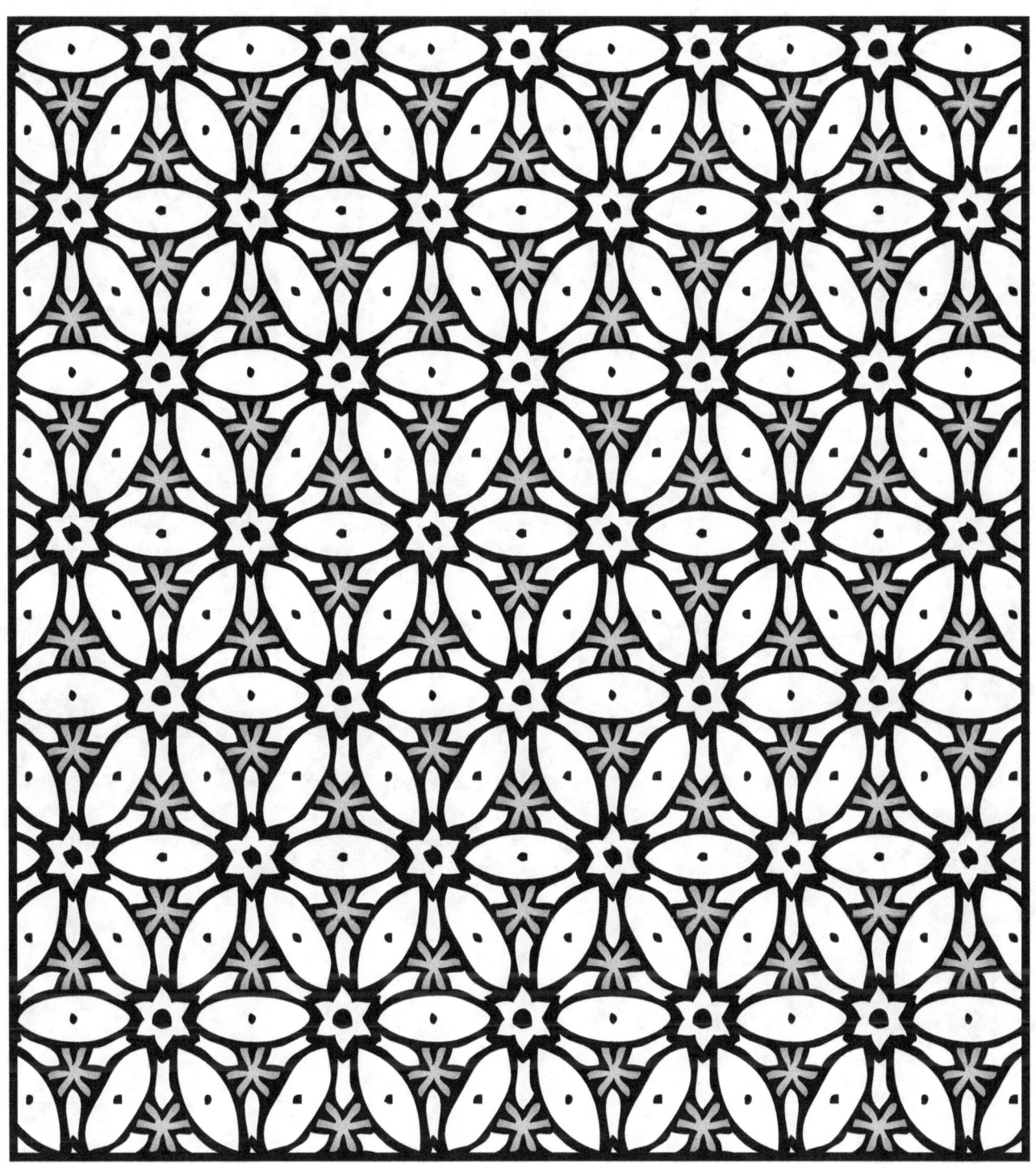

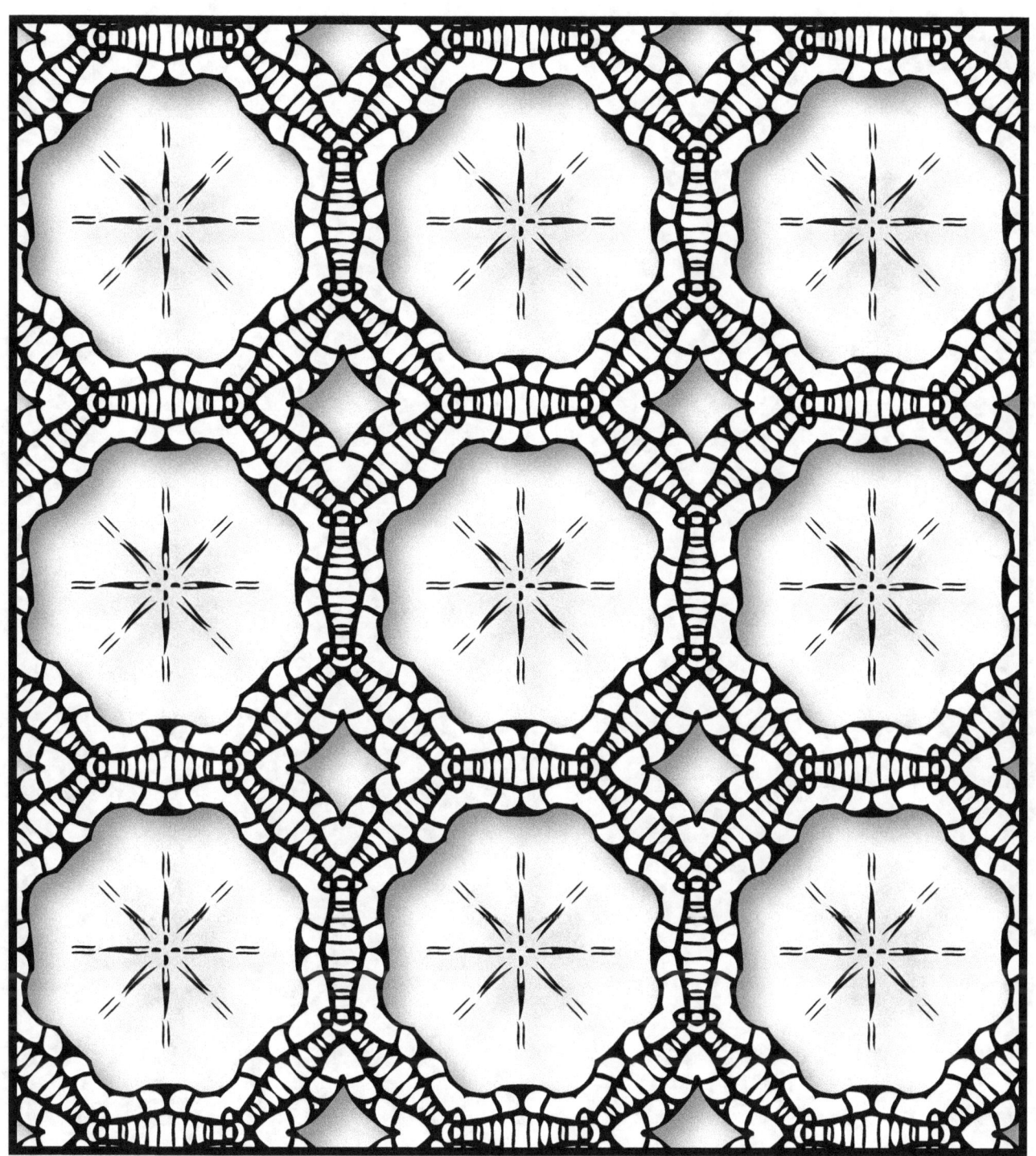

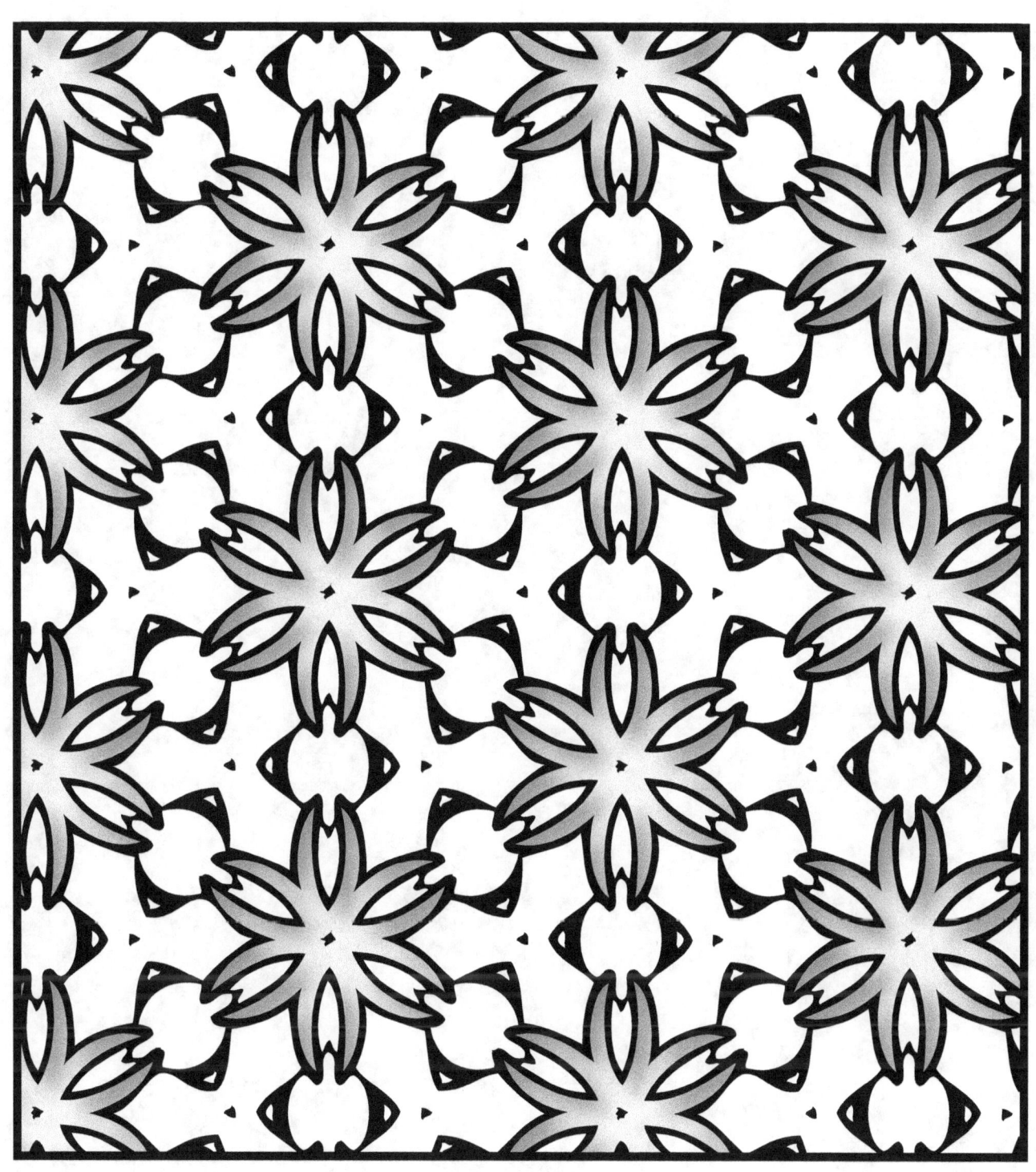

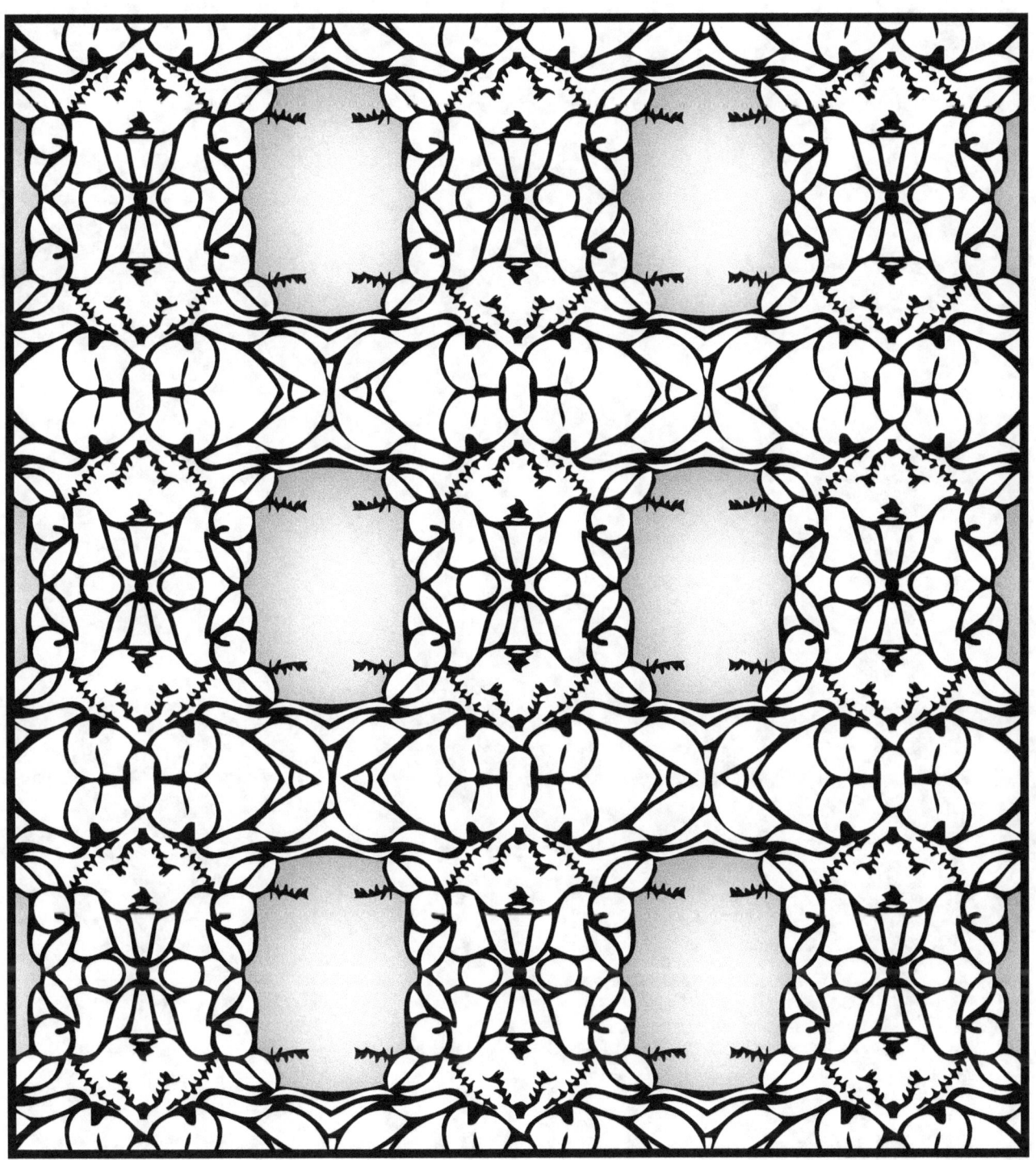

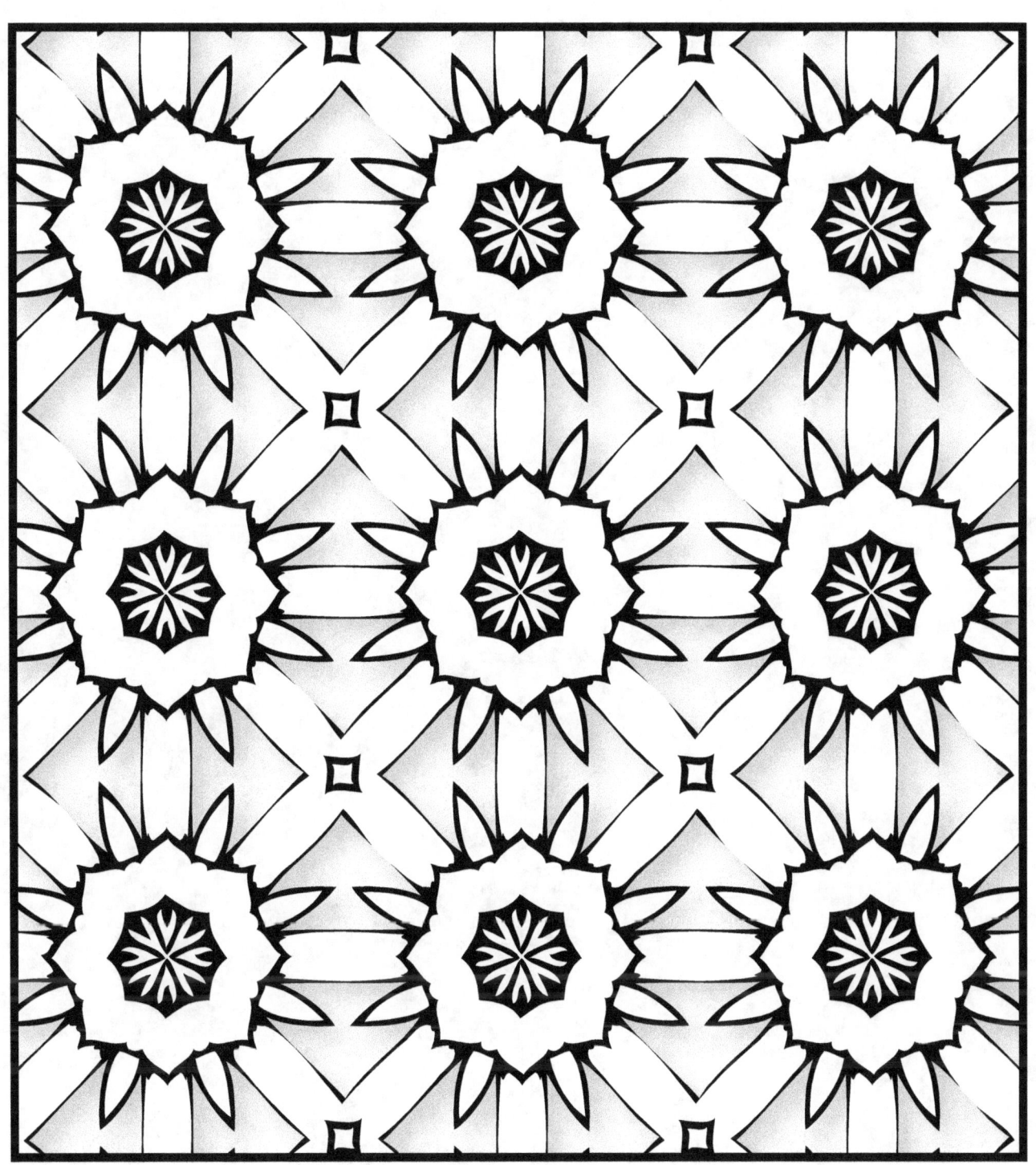

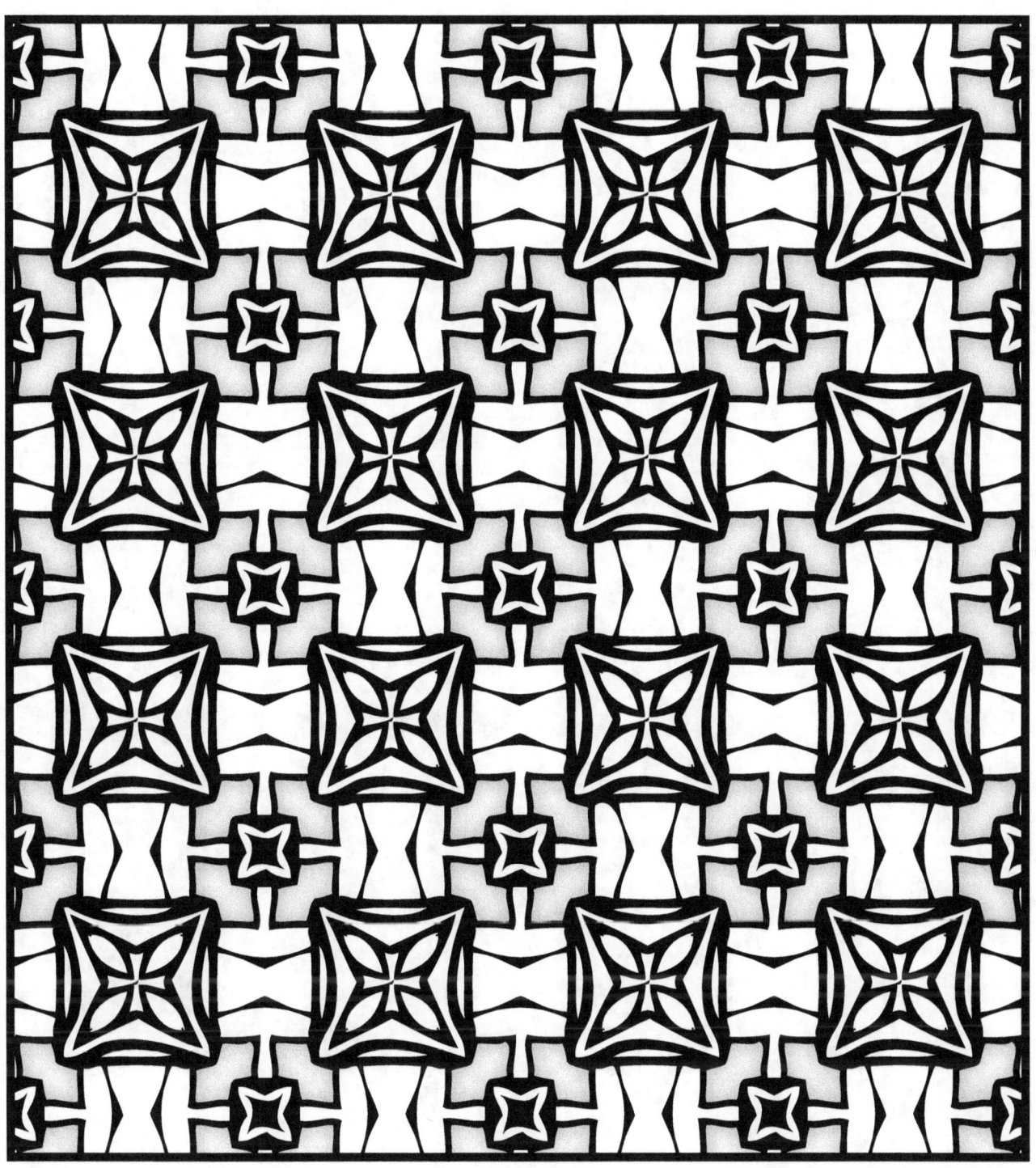

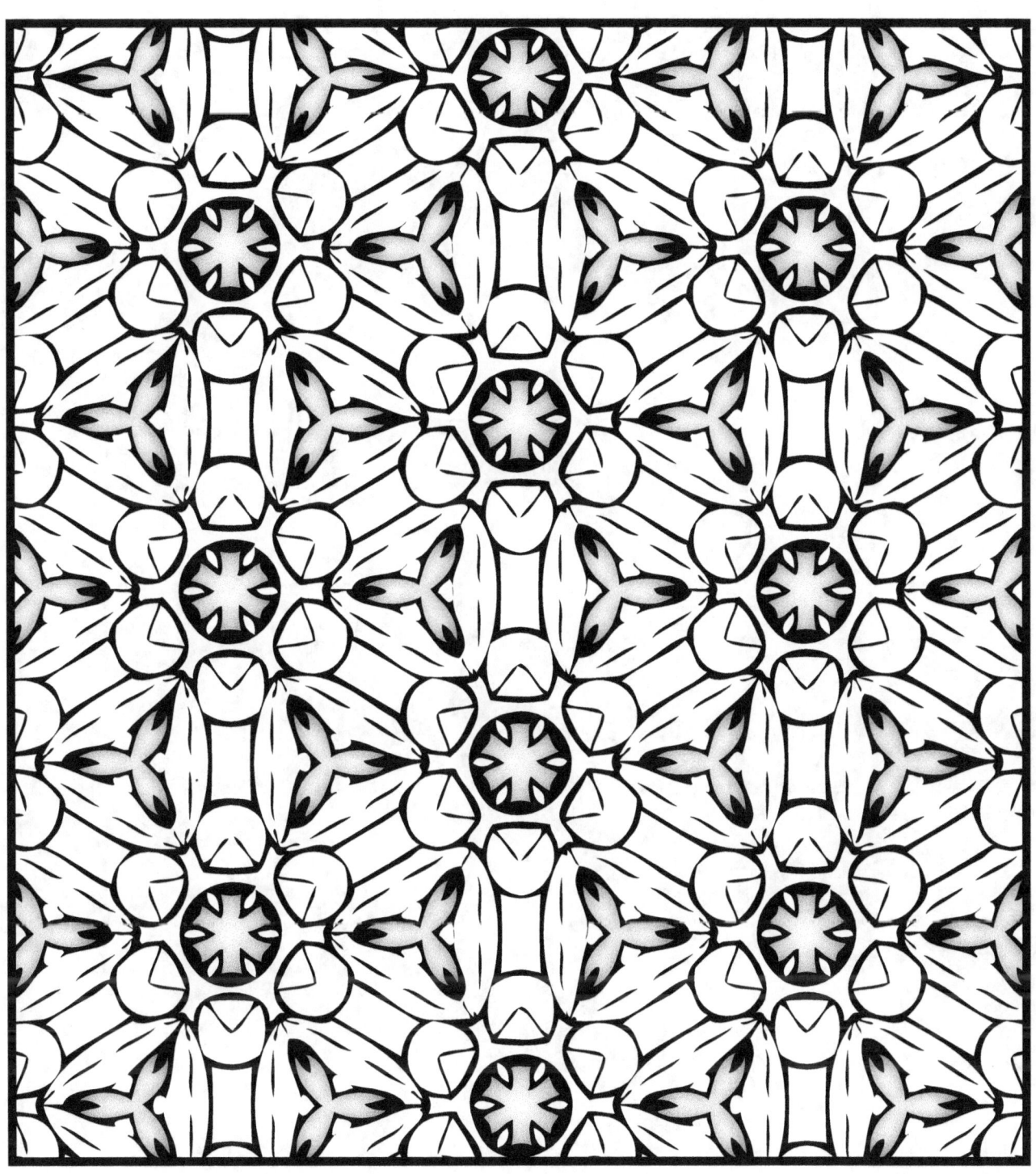

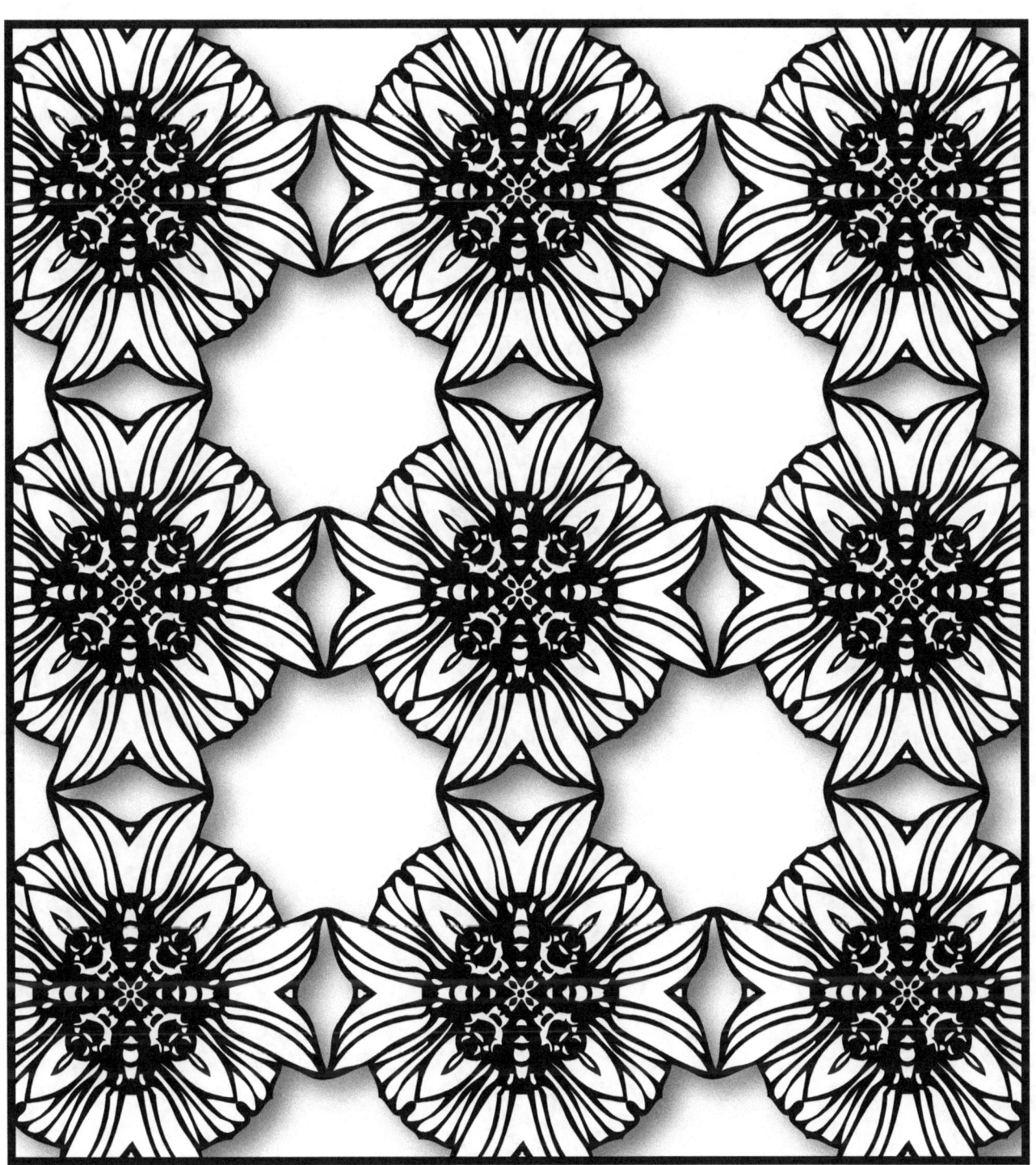

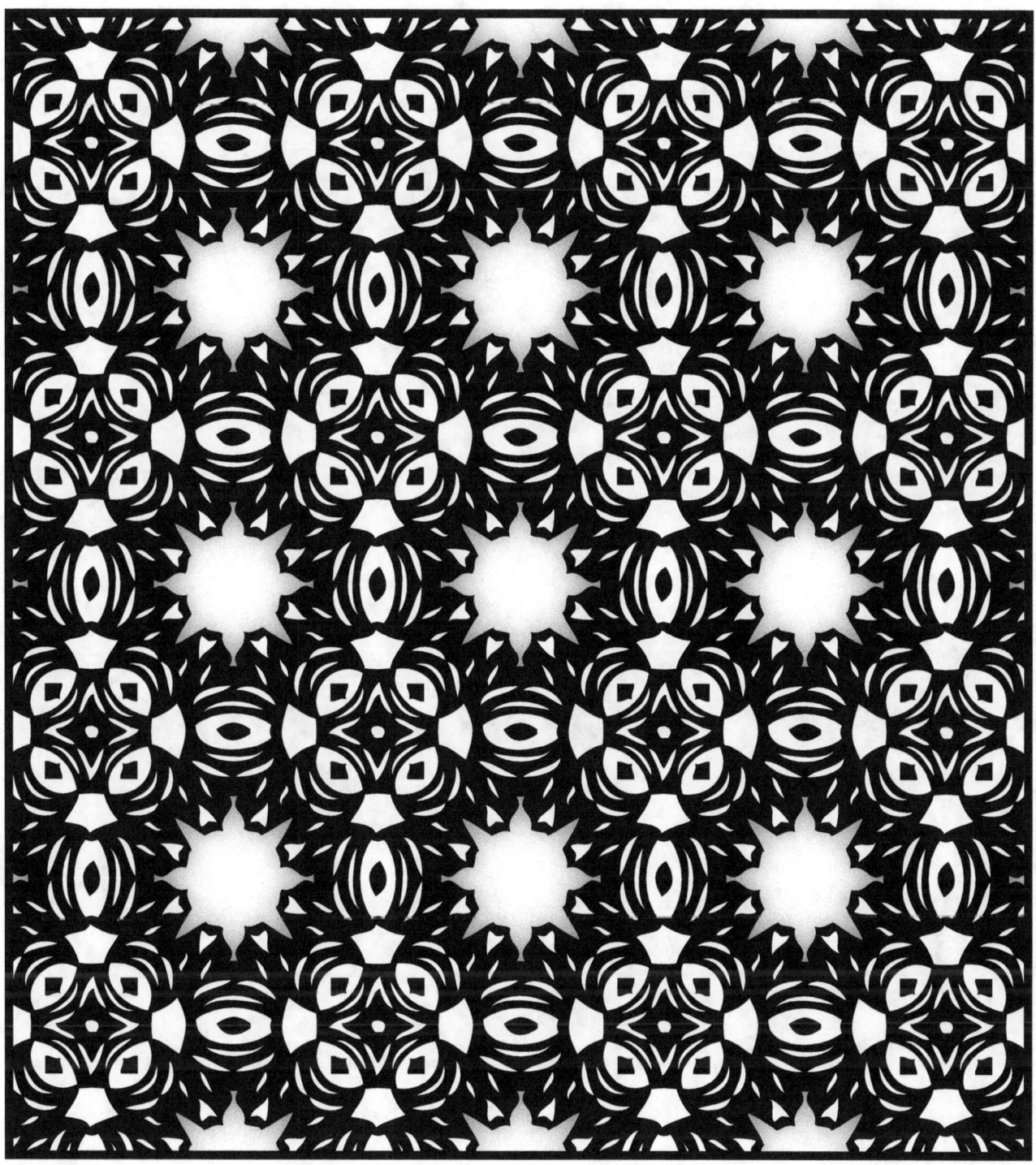

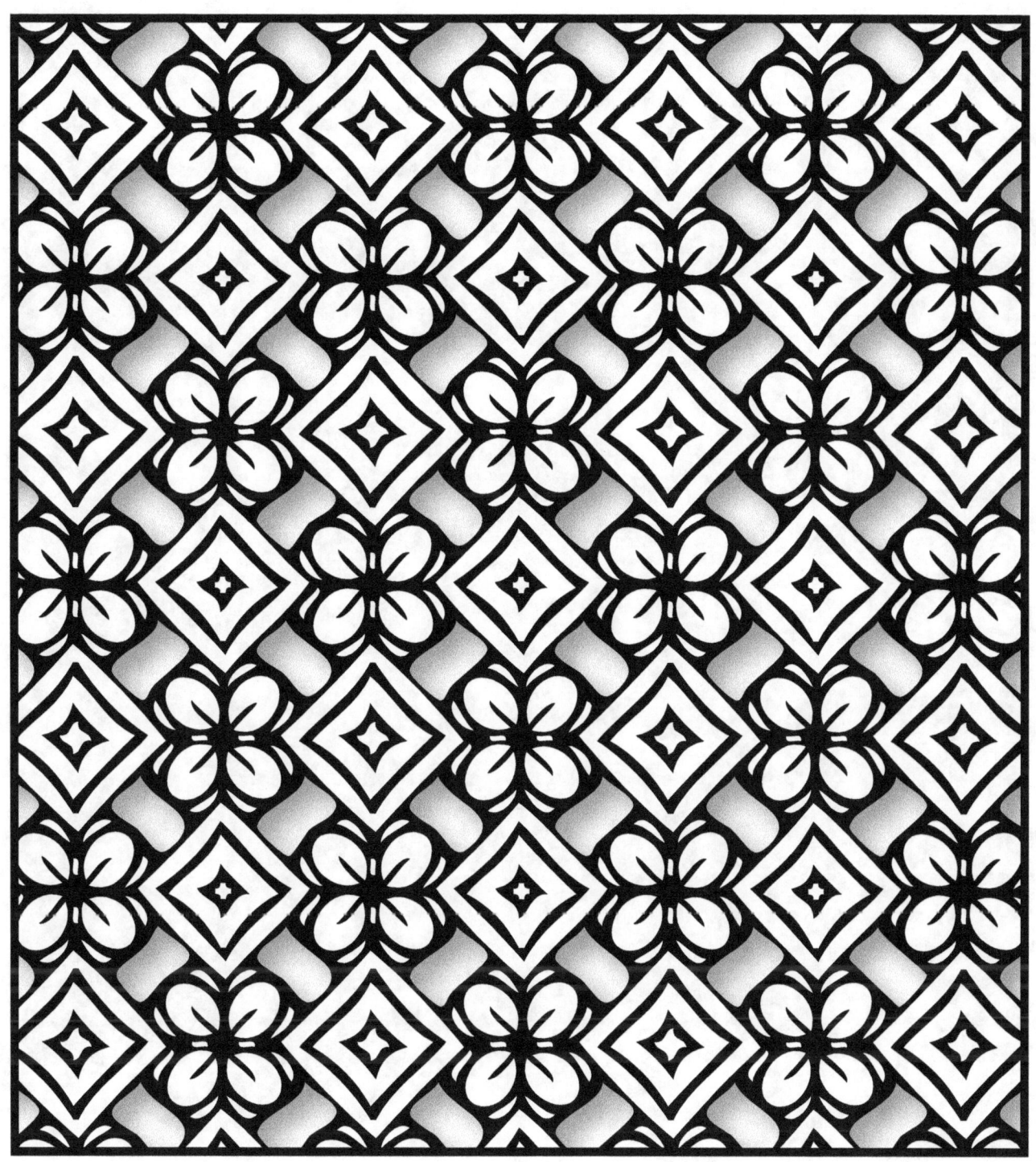

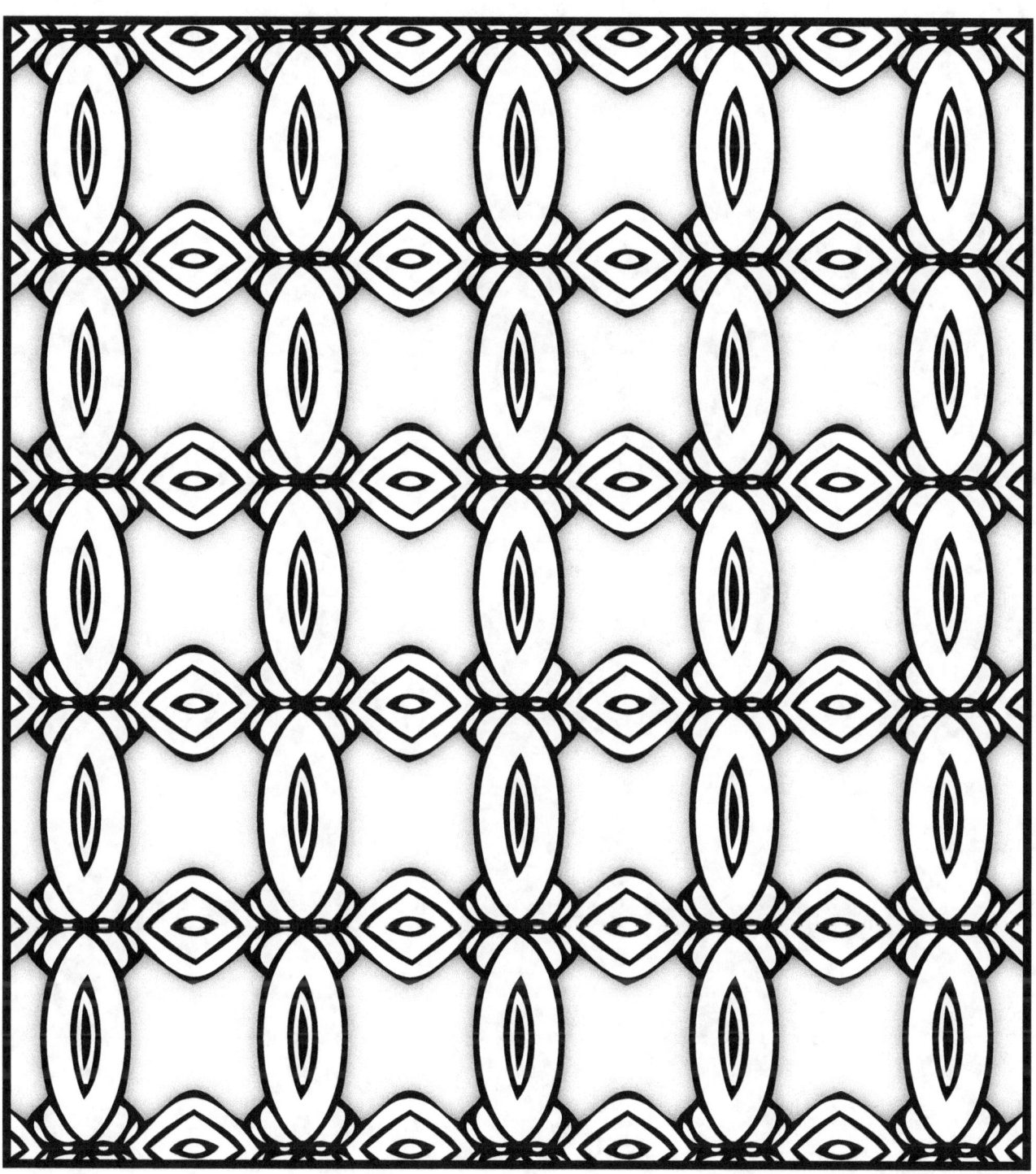

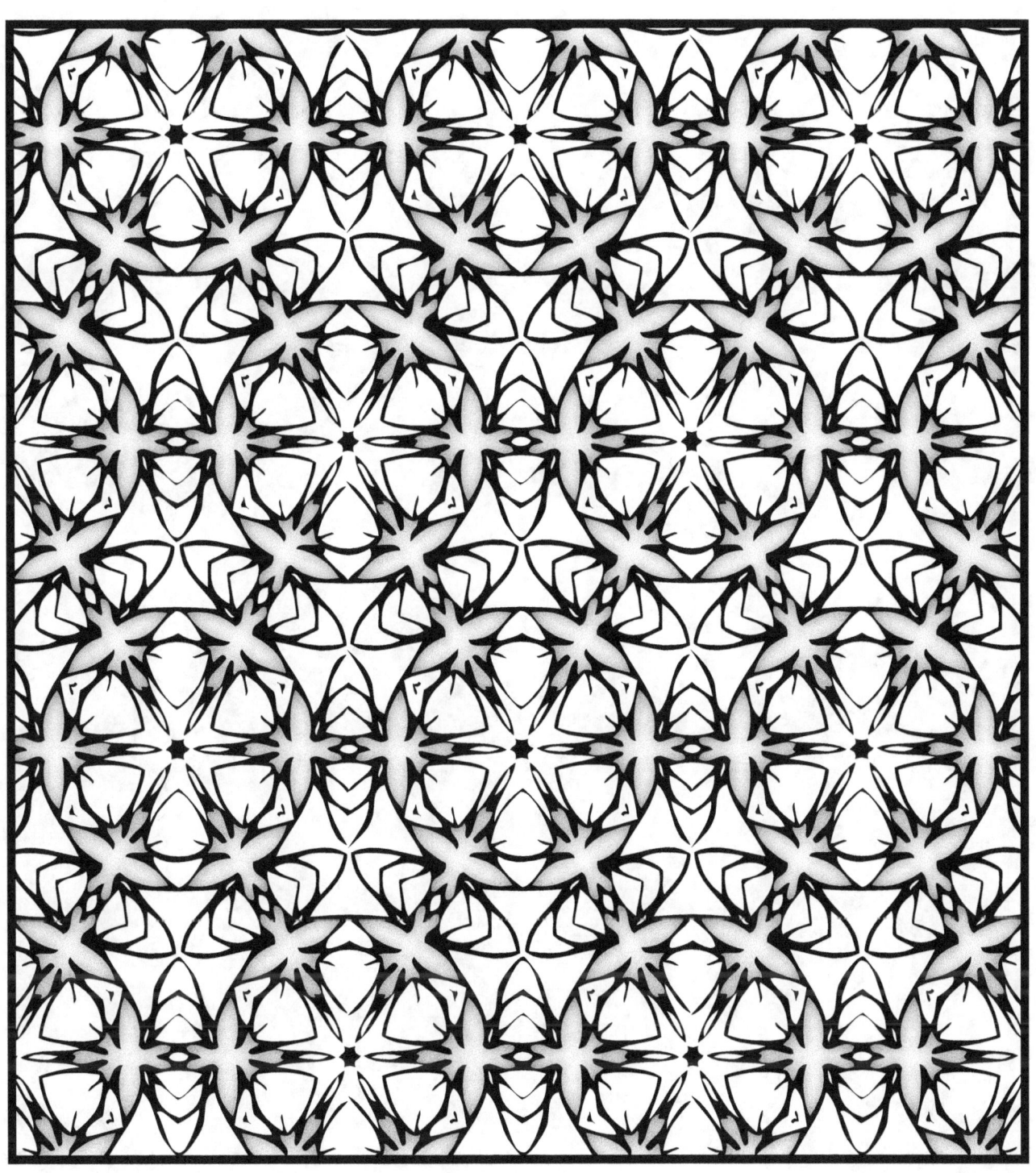

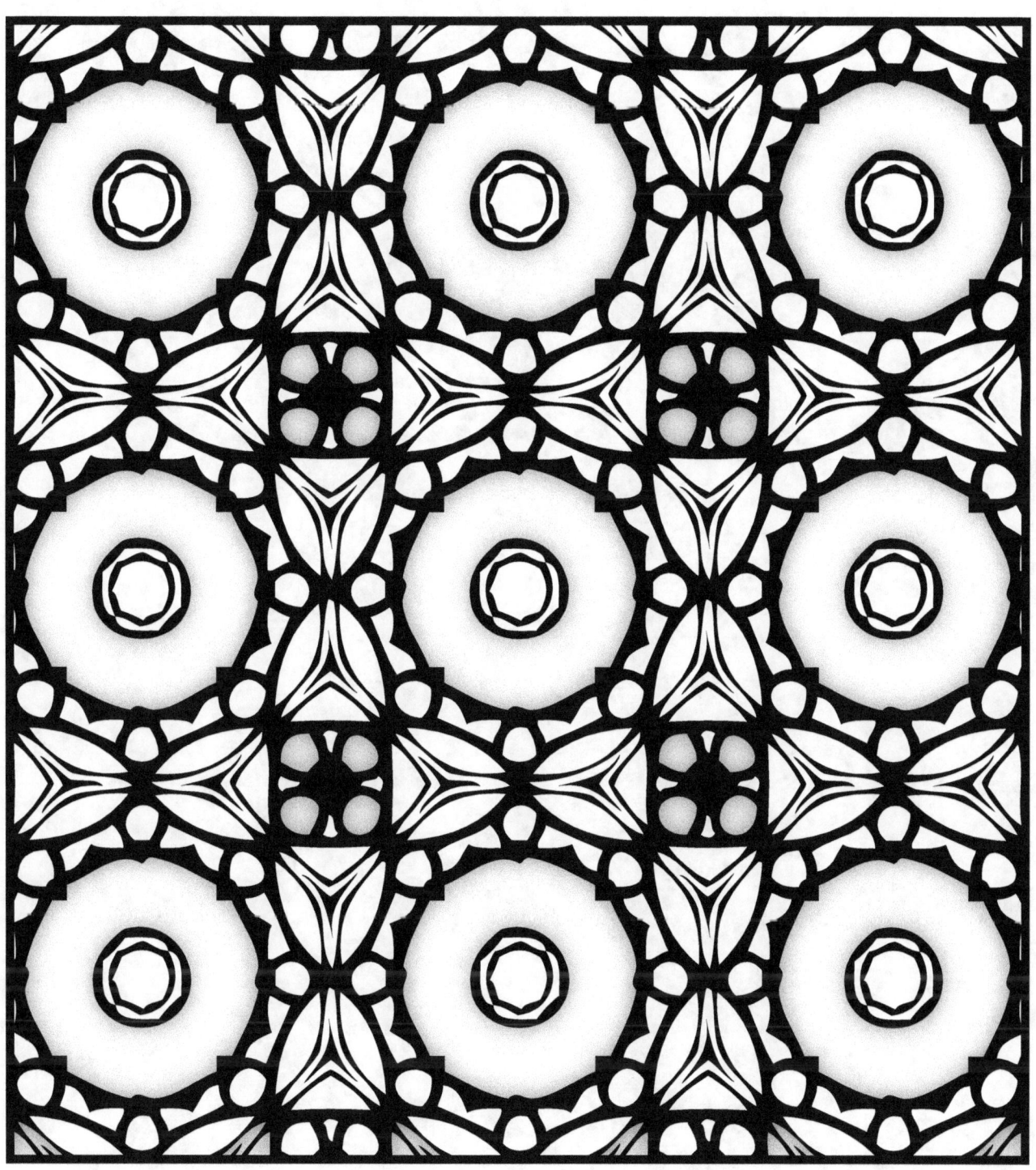

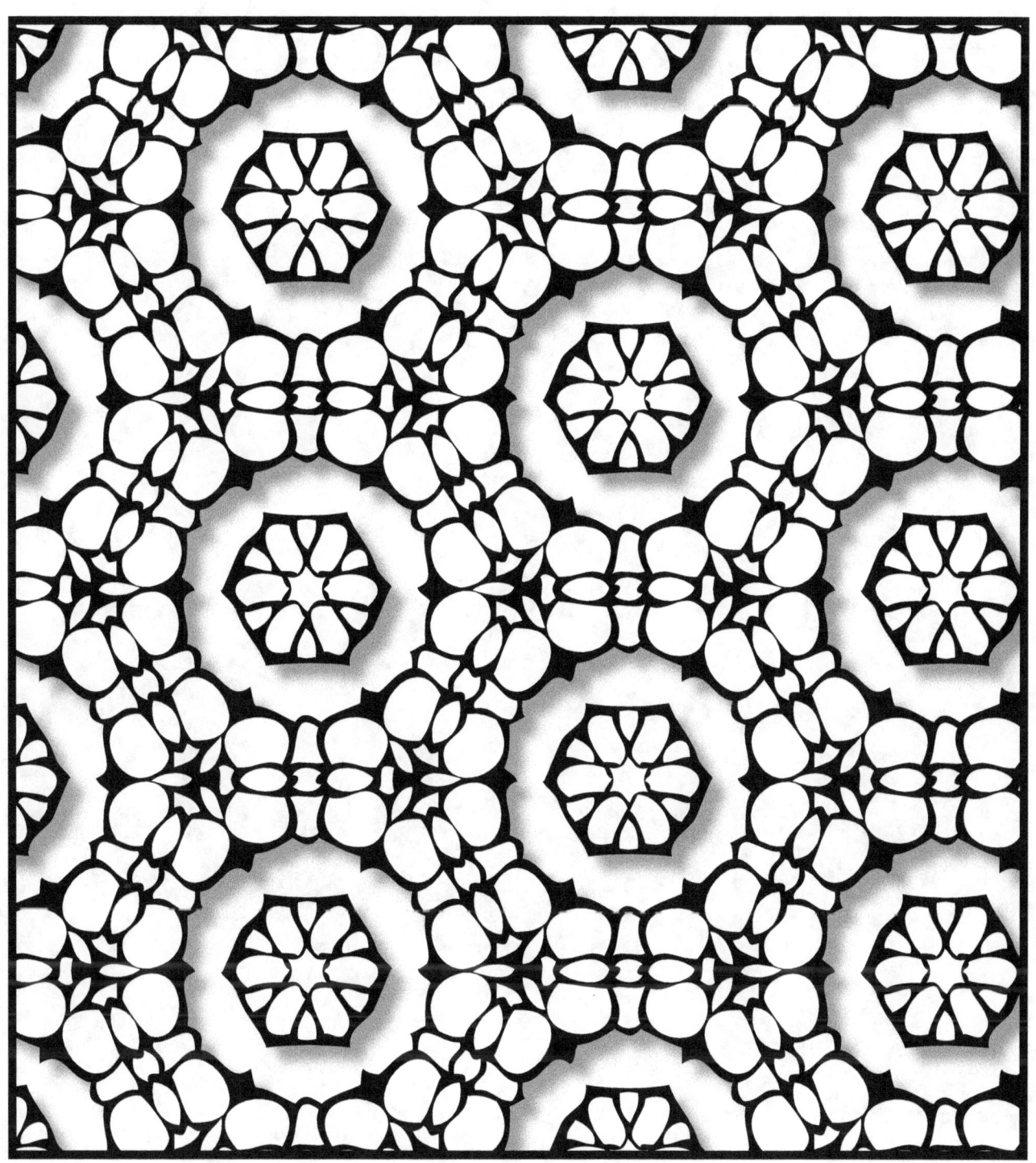

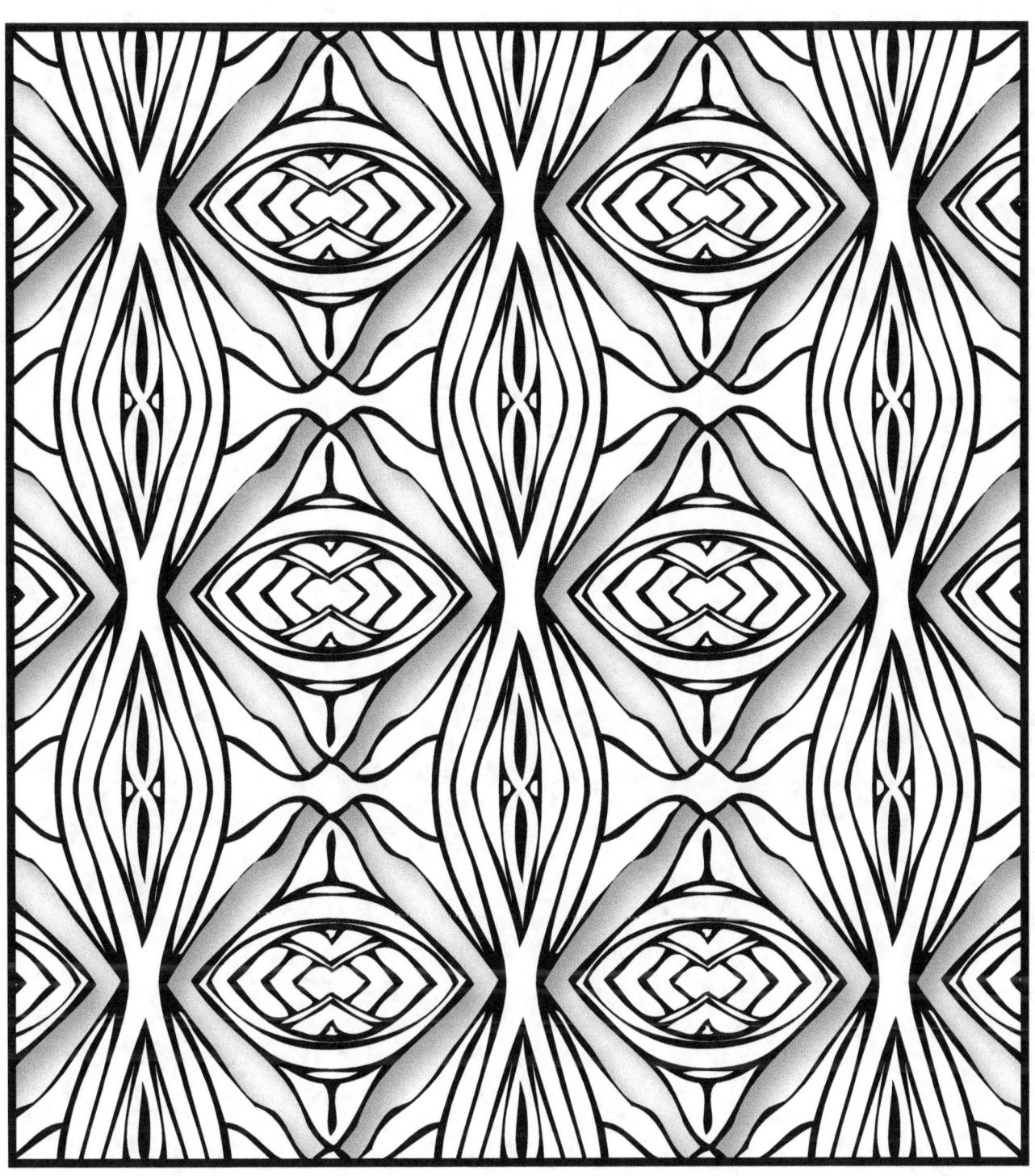

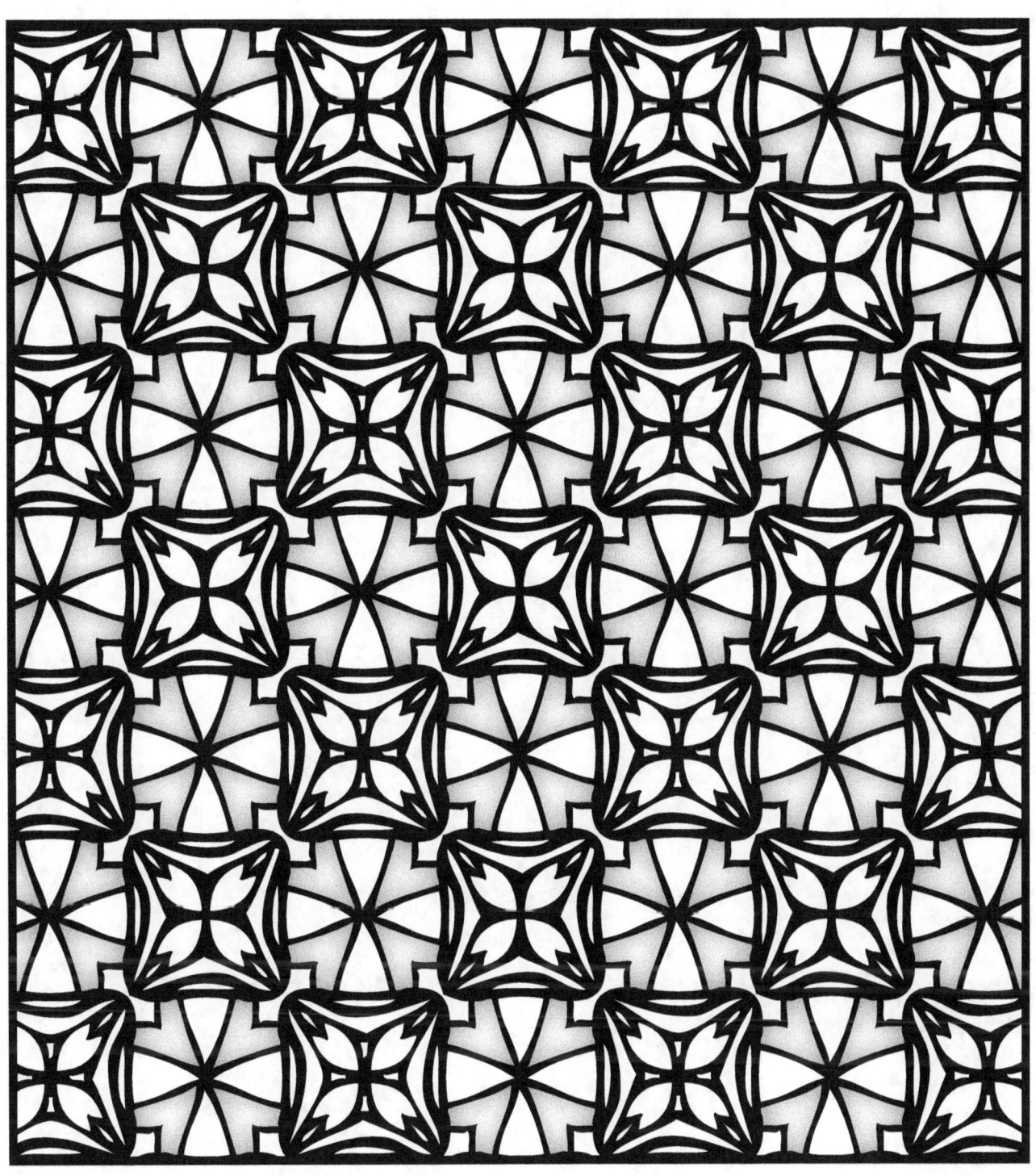

COLOR SWATCH TEST PAGE

Use this page to test and reference your colors

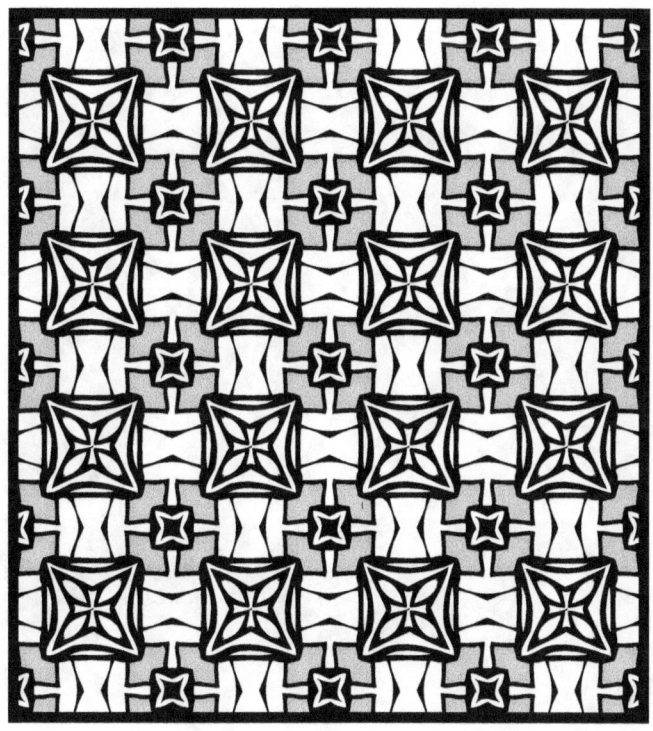

Shadowboxes Coloring Book
© 2016 Paula Parrish

www.lovelyleisure.me

www.ingramcontent.com/pod-product-compliance
Lightning Source LLC
Chambersburg PA
CBHW080934170526
45158CB00008B/2291